ARCHITECTURAL SALVAGE

A Guide to Selecting, Buying and Using Reclaimed Building Materials

ARCHITECTURAL SALVAGE

A Guide to Selecting, Buying and Using Reclaimed Building Materials

Geoffrey David West

THE CROWOOD PRESS

First published in 2010 by
The Crowood Press Ltd
Ramsbury, Marlborough
Wiltshire SN8 2HR

www.crowood.com

British Library Cataloguing-in-Publication Data
A catalogue record for this book is available from the British Library.

ISBN 978 1 84797 207 1

Disclaimer
All tools and equipment used in connection with architectural salvage should be operated in strict accordance with both the current health and safety regulations and the manufacturer's instructions. The author and publisher do not accept any responsibility or liability of any kind in any manner whatsoever for any error or omission, or any loss, damage, injury or adverse outcome incurred as result of the use of any of the information contained in this book, or reliance upon it. If in doubt about any aspect of architectural salvage readers are advised to seek professional advice. The fact that particular salvage dealers' businesses are mentioned in this publication does not indicate that either the publishers, or the author, are necessarily recommending them in preference to any other salvage dealers, which are not mentioned herein.

Acknowledgements
I would like to thank Richie Harkness for his help with IT issues, and also the many salvage yards who kindly allowed me to wander around taking photographs of their stock. In particular Adrian Burrows, of Abbots Bridge Home & Garden Renovation Centre, Peter Watson, of Cox's Architectural Salvage Yard, Debbie Kedge and Steve Tomlin of Minchinhampton Architectural Salvage Co (MASCo) Ltd, Amanda Garrett and Anthony Reeve of LASSCO Three Pigeons, Jason and Nadine Davis, of Architectural Forum, Phil Wilson and Daniel Payne of Victorian Woodworks and all staff at Architectural Salvage Source, Mongers Architectural Salvage and Heritage Reclamations (all company details at back of book). Special thanks to the following, whose items are pictured on the front and back covers: Heritage Reclamations, Mongers Architectural Salvage, MASCo Architectural Salvage Yard, LASSCO Ltd, Cox's Architectural Salvage Yard and Abbots Bridge Home and Garden Renovation Centre. Plus all the people in the salvage trade who have spoken to me over the years and allowed me to reproduce their ideas and advice. And love and thanks to Olga for her help and support.

Typeset by Jean Cussons Typesetting, Diss, Norfolk

Printed and bound in Malaysia by Times Offset (M) Sdn Bhd

Contents

CHAPTER I

Why Buy Second-Hand Materials?

A good reason for buying second-hand building items is that if you live in an old property, materials of the same vintage are more likely to be in keeping than modern products; not only will they match, but their surface 'ageing' will blend better with the building. There are several other points in their favour: old materials, in particular wood, were often of better quality than are new ones, and manufacturing craftsmanship was definitely of a higher standard – there are very few hand skills used when making building materials in these days of mechanization.

There is also the ecological argument, that using up the earth's space to put non-degenerative

Nadine Davis, cheerfully taking stock of the items in the yard of Architectural Forum, which she runs with her husband Jason. (Courtesy Architectural Forum)

View of Architectural Forum's yard – fascinating items everywhere you look! (Courtesy Architectural Forum)

materials into landfill, while also using resources to make something similar, uses up energy unnecessarily. Admittedly timber will naturally degenerate, as will metals to some extent, but few other construction materials will blend into the soil in the foreseeable future, if ever. And if you are buying reclaimed building materials for a period house from a local salvage yard, then vernacular aspects, such as the colour and texture of stone or bricks, are likely to be in sympathy with your home. The trade in reclaimed materials only began to take off around thirty years ago, but it has been flourishing ever since.

In the past, second-hand materials were usually cheaper than new products, but now that is not, generally, the case. Just as with the antique trade, rarity value increasingly means that genuine old items are often more expensive than those fresh from the builders' merchant. Throughout the fol-

lowing pages I have tried to give a very approximate indication of which items are more expensive to buy new than second-hand and vice versa, and by how much. Products which until a few years ago were simply not made any more, such as roll-top baths and cast-iron chimneypieces, are now being produced as 'reproduction' items. Nowadays the standard of reproductions of certain pieces can be excellent, so much so that they can sometimes be hard to tell from the real thing; alternatively they can be awful, and instantly recognizable as cheap facsimiles.

As an example of fine modern craftsmanship Thomas Crapper Ltd, who make reproduction sanitary equipment and taps, have bought the company name of the original Thomas Crapper, sanitary engineers, and now make the items in the same way as they were made in Victorian times, using the same moulds; therefore these items have exactly the same quality of finish as the originals. Likewise, Christopher Wray Lighting make reproduction lamps and light fittings, some of which are made in the same way as the originals. This kind of reproduction – when the original tools and moulds are used – is called 'replication' or 'continuous production' rather than 'reproduction', and replicated pieces are, necessarily, expensive, to take into account the excellent craftsmanship and attention to detail. There are also companies making taps, door furniture, chimneypieces and all kinds of other items that are of an extremely high standard.

To condemn something as a reproduction does not necessarily mean it is of inferior quality or appearance. The general rule of thumb is that if a firm is making reproduction items in a similar way to how they were originally made, the product is likely to be of good quality, and its price will justifiably reflect this. It is also an increasing trend that salvage dealers very often also manufacture some reproduction items themselves, as an adjunct to their main business, usually as a way of enhancing the antique items they sell. One example is bathroom fittings. Salvage dealers who professionally restore centuries-old baths might make reproduction taps for them, and also may cast the occasional missing foot for a roll-top bath or make a reproduction cistern for an antique loo (usually in aluminium, which looks similar to cast iron).

When assessing these non-twenty-first-century items, whether genuine or reproduction, there is no point in giving any price comparisons, because the general rule is that good, top quality reproductions will cost about the same as second-hand antique examples that have been expertly renovated. Bad quality reproductions ought to be much cheaper, and one of the key aims of this book is to show you how to distinguish between good reproductions, bad reproductions and genuine antiques, so that you can make an informed decision about whether to pay what is being asked. Reputable dealers will, of course, tell you if an item is genuine or reproduction; a valuable antique item may even have written provenance, or other evidence of where it has come from.

Many building materials are incredibly long lasting, ironically the very reason that they're unsuitable for landfill. The Normans used thousand-year-old Roman bricks to build with, and many of these buildings are still standing. Glass is known to last at least two thousand years. Clay tiles can be less resilient: they may delaminate (split into layers), as can slates. But stone blocks are timeless (there is a 2,000 million-year-old stone in Chislehurst in Kent).

The remaining materials to consider are timber and metals. The oldest timbers used in Britain were oak and elm. Unfortunately very little elm has survived, but plenty of good rock-hard 500-year-old oak is still in existence, both in buildings and in salvage yards. Pine, imported from the Baltic continuously after 1700, gradually replaced the older indigenous timbers from that time onwards, and because it was usually painted to protect its surface, a great deal of this timber is still perfectly serviceable: indeed the term 'softwood' is almost a misnomer, because this old pine, up until the nineteenth century, was largely of heartwood, it was thoroughly seasoned, and its parent trees were very long-lived. As a result this old timber is much harder and more stable than the warp-prone softwood you can buy today.

The merits of ancient wrought iron and Victorian cast iron are examined later on, but these metals are definitely more beautiful, and in many ways more durable, than modern steel; if protected by paint, wrought iron and cast iron can last for many hundreds of years.

Surprisingly there are those who, in principle, dislike the concept of using second-hand building materials. Amongst these are some members of The Society for the Protection of Ancient Buildings (SPAB). This is an excellent organization with a fine history, and they have done wonderful work for many years in saving old buildings from neglect. Begun by the great William Morris and other notable members of the pre-Raphaelite brotherhood in 1877 to try and prevent over-zealous Victorian developers from renovating or 'restoring' away the character of medieval buildings, SPAB believes in looking after old buildings at all costs. SPAB established the practice of 'listing' historically important buildings as a way of legally protecting them from wanton destruction or alteration by

Huge entrance portico to a public building – the kind of salvage item that looks absolutely splendid, and you feel you've just got to try and find a home for it. (Courtesy LASSCO Ltd)

Another huge entrance portico.
(Courtesy LASSCO Ltd)

Yet another entrance to what must have been an amazing building. (Courtesy LASSCO Ltd)

their owners. Listed buildings enjoy legal protection, and owners have to apply for listed building consent to alter or repair them; this application is handled by a conservation officer (CO) within the town council planning department. If your building is listed it is very important to discuss any plans you may have for restoration or making changes with your local CO, and ideally to form a friendly relationship with them.

SPAB is a great organization and I would recommend anyone with an old house to join. It's like a friendly helpful 'club', and offers an advice line, lectures, homeowners' courses of all kinds (including those in practical crafts), plus a fantastic range of up-to-date technical pamphlets and books; what's more, if you're looking for an old house they have a list of properties for sale, as well as an active 'mills' section, for looking after derelict mills.

Similarly it can be a good idea to join one of the other amenity societies (The Victorian Society, The Georgian Group, The Twentieth Century Society), all of whom also offer literature, courses, lectures, advice, information and support.

In SPAB's opinion, reusing second-hand building materials encourages theft of such items from healthy houses: for instance lead is stolen from roofs, or fireplaces may be ripped out from abandoned homes. Instead of reusing old materials, SPAB believes it's important to train the craftspeople of today to make building materials as they used to be made, thus encouraging new industries, skills and crafts. (In SPAB's stated 'purpose' they say that 'Trade in salvaged building materials encourages the destruction of old buildings, whereas demand for the same materials new helps keep them in production.') This is a reasonable viewpoint, but in many people's opinion, is dependent on theory rather than practicalities. Certainly in the early days there may have been unethical salvage dealers who might knowingly have dealt in plundered building materials, but nowadays the Salvo code (see below) has done much to remove this trade.

The police have also tightened up on unlawful trading of this kind. In December 2003 the Dealing in Cultural Objects (Offences) Act became law, which stated that it will be an offence punishable by up to seven years in prison for a UK dealer, or an overseas dealer on a buying trip to the UK, to be caught dishonestly complicit in the sale of objects unlawfully removed from listed buildings or gardens. In addition to risking prosecution, any salvage dealer who is caught handling stolen goods loses the goods in addition to losing the money he has paid for them; so while the overwhelming majority of dealers are honest, the few who are not are going to be deterred far more than they used to be.

As for the ecological argument, here is an extract from a letter written by Amanda Garrett of LASSCO Three Pigeons, to their local MP, reproduced with the company's permission:

… The EU 2008 Waste Framework Directive requires that planning authorities are given positive guidance to ensure reusable material is reclaimed for reuse when demolition, alteration, refurbishment or restoration takes place. Did you know, for example, that every year the UK demolishes around three billion bricks, and significant fossil energy is used to crush these. This failure to reuse means additional carbon emissions are emitted from new brick manufacture as well as the emission produced by the crushing of old bricks. What a bad use of energy and resource efficiency I am sure you would agree. …

MASCo's yard is huge, and there are also several vast indoor showroom areas. If you can't find it here, you're unlikely to find it anywhere. (Courtesy MASCo Architectural Salvage Yard)

Mongers yard entrance. Mongers have a splendid shop showroom, full of incredibly beautiful items, and outside, all the rough-and-tough outdoor/garden-type things you could possibly want.
(Courtesy Mongers Architectural Salvage)

There is an organization called Salvo that has been providing information on antique and reclaimed materials for buildings and gardens since 1992. It acts as a networking tool for dealers in the trade, and also to disseminate information to the public, and offers an extremely useful 'Wants and Offers' service on its website (www.salvo.co.uk), whereby you can simply type in what you are looking for in the 'For Sale' section, and find a number of dealers (or individuals) who are offering such items. Dealers who are members of Salvo sign up to the 'Salvo Code', established in 1995, for traders who wanted to make a positive stand about good practice in stock purchasing. Traders signing up to the code agree that they will only handle items

they are confident are from buildings that have been (or are being) demolished. This code now has supporting businesses in various countries in Europe and in North America. The 'Salvo Theft Alert System' informs dealers and the police about thefts and past stolen items. www.theftalerts.com is now available for independent use by publishers, police, insurers and heritage groups. (It is important to stress that a great many reputable salvage dealers do not happen to be Salvo members, perhaps because they have been trading successfully for many years without wanting to join an organization.)

One other interesting thing: for many years I have been writing for the magazines *Period Living* and *Period House and its Garden* (both of which are fascinating reading, and which I can highly recommend to anyone who is interested in all aspects of owning an old house), and in the course of writing articles on reclaimed materials I have been phoning different salvage yards to ask for advice and information. I have found without exception that the characters I speak to are friendly, helpful and likeable. They are the kind of people who will go the extra mile to help you, generally individualists who love old buildings. Everyone has always been prepared to chat to me for many hours, as evidenced by the 'expert quotes' in this book – and when receiving this free advice, I wasn't even buying anything! If you go and have a chat with someone at a salvage yard, they're likely to take an interest in whatever you're doing, give you as much help and information as they can, and they won't hesitate to recommend another dealer if they haven't got what you want. The salvage trade is a friendly trade, and many of its practitioners know each other and help reciprocally whenever possible. Finally, never be afraid to bargain – they won't be offended and they can always refuse your offer.

All the practical advice for using second-hand materials given hereafter is given in good faith, bearing in mind that no responsibility can be taken for any damage to property or personal injury suffered as a result. When using tools, especially power tools, and/or if you are working at heights, always observe all the relevant safety issues, and wear protective safety equipment – for example eye, ear and hand protection. Salvage yards can be dangerous places, particularly for children, as heavy items can fall and there are lorries and equipment around, so always make sure they are with you at all times.

Now to hand over to some of the people who have made this book possible.

EXPERT QUOTES

Thornton Kay, salvage consultant and creator and proprietor of Salvo

Nowadays conservation bodies preserve old buildings, of course, but in the 1970s, having destroyed many Georgian terraces, Bath City Council was still trying to demolish its own listed buildings. After studying architecture in the 1970s I worked as a conservation builder and was there, in the front line, trying to prevent (and succeeding in two instances – Green Park Station and The Real Tennis Courts) the demolition of some fine old buildings! We set up one of Britain's first salvage yards to rescue as much as we could from the demolitions, and started trying to persuade the public to buy these old materials so at least they weren't gone for ever.

In order to restore and repair the architectural salvage we developed workshops for different trades, with artists and craftspeople who developed skills in areas such as marble work, woodwork and metal. A lot of these traditional skills were started from scratch. There were no places where they were taught in those days, and few old craftspeople who knew the old ways of doing things. The skills had to be relearned.

Fifteen years later, after encouragement from conservation organizations, reproduction items began to be manufactured, mainly in China, as a substitute for the real thing. Replica items are often inferior to the original antique and reclaimed material. Victorian pine was logged from the indigenous first growth forests of British Columbia, from majestic slow-growing 500-year-old trees, for instance, far superior to modern plantation pines. And the Victorian era was the pinnacle of craft skills. Of course, the Victorians of the industrial age developed machines to supplement hand labour, but really in most areas of the supply of materials for building during the Georgian and Victorian periods, decorative construction materials have never been bettered. Generally, repro is getting better, some of extraordinarily high quality, but in my opinion, still falling short of the originals (although some are so good that it's hard to tell them from the originals).

In the early days we were architectural salvage heroes rescuing stuff from demolition and landfill, but gradually, as we created a business around the ethos, some conservationists began to resent our activities. If you establish a second-hand market in something, you're also creating a market for possibly stolen items. Yes, theft of second-hand building materials did increase in the 1980s, because the market boomed, but it is largely now under control and self-policed by the trade. Salvo and its members and other honest members of our profession are trying to curb this as much as we possibly can. Very few stolen items are in salvage yards, as far as we are aware. As for the market in second-hand materials encouraging unnecessary demolition, there has never, to my knowledge, been a building demolished in order to cull the materials – in fact quite the reverse. 33,000 tons a day of reclaimable materials are still going to landfill! No demolition contractor is going to demolish the building just to get the materials out. There are various apocryphal stories fed to the press by conservation societies to say this has occurred, but when I have looked at the specific cases, every one, without exception, has been proved to be inaccurate.

The third objection to the trade is that it's said that it has obstructed the traditional manufacture of the new materials – for example that the trade in reclaimed pantiles has hindered the encouragement of a new traditional pantile manufacturing industry. This is completely spurious. In every single instance of manufacture of traditional materials, it has been the reclaimed market that has actually spawned the reproduction market. Take bricks: in the 1970s we used to reclaim handmade bricks, because you couldn't buy them. New handmade brick manufacture has taken off since that market was developed by the reclamation industry – and now they sell into that market. Several brickmakers even produce ranges of new looka-like machine-made tinted 'reclaimed' bricks. What's more, the salvage market, because of the massive demands for repair and restoration at the top end, creates a whole artisan class of very, very good restorers and fine craftsmen and women. Gavin Stamp, one of Britain's leading architectural historians, once said that the salvage industry of Britain is a happy consequence of the profligacy of the construction industry in Britain towards its buildings.

What are the advantages of using second-hand materials to repair your home? If you've got an old house and you use old materials, you'll add value to it. If you use a builder or architect, the overall job may cost you more, because these people find it quicker to use new materials, so they may charge more for their extra time and trouble – they may be learning about reclaimed materials at your expense. However, anyone doing a DIY building job will usually save a lot of money by using second-hand materials, and perhaps be able to do a better job. In some sectors of the market, such as antique door furniture, supply is no longer readily available, but demand continues apace, so it's reasonable to expect reproduction.

I would say that in practically every instance where you use reclaimed materials, you will be helping to reduce global warming and CO_2 emissions, and you'll be preserving some historic old building resources. Likewise, in practically every instance where you're using mass-manufactured new materials, you are destroying resources, helping to increase global warming and making the planet worse. Of course it is not very realistic (although possible) to do a building job using entirely reclaimed and antique materials – 90 per cent of what you're going to use is going to be new. A good target, however, would be to use 10 per cent of reclaimed materials rather than 1 per cent, which is the national average. If I were going to build an ultra-modern house, I'd still use old materials, but in a modern way. An increasing number of architects are beginning to use modern, good quality materials alongside old ones, for the contrast, and it can look great.

Salvo is not a trade association for the salvage trade. We don't claim to represent the trade and their views. Salvage traders are essentially very much individuals, with their own distinct interests, talents and ideas. For many years I suggested to them they might like to form a trade association of reclamation dealers, which up to now they have not, although there are possible signs that this might happen in 2010. Salvo started a voluntary code for dealers – the Salvo Code – in 1995.

Steve Haycock, Dorset Reclamation

The quality of reproductions has certainly improved over the years, but there are things that can't be copied. Like the fantastic finish you get on

ABOVE: Abbots Bridge Home & Garden Renovation Centre. Like MASCo, Abbots have a huge outside area, and their main showroom is on two floors of a vast building.
(Courtesy Abbots Bridge Home & Garden Renovation Centre)

RIGHT: Cox's Architectural Salvage Yard. One of those marvellous places where you never know what you might find.
(Courtesy Cox's Architectural Salvage Yard)

really old flagstones – the patina that can only be created by something being walked on for hundreds of years. It's the same with old ironwork. We once sold a fifteenth-century doorknocker – handmade wrought iron overlaid with silver. The customer who bought it put it on her door, and had strangers knocking to ask where she'd got it from! Old cast iron is different from the new castings – the ore used is not the same. And the nice lichen finish you get on old stone, such as you find on the old stone troughs, that's what you cannot replicate. There are a lot of reproductions made in mild steel of items that were originally made in wrought iron. Although they look much the same now, in ten years' time they'll be rusting away, while the antique will not, and it will always look beautiful.

If you're unsure about something there isn't a single reclamation yard I know of that isn't prepared to give advice. Most yards have got someone who knows about fireplaces or bathrooms, things like that. Nearly every dealer will have things that no other dealer will have. Every day you get to handle absolutely amazing, lovely things. Every dealer has their own special interest – mine happens to be door furniture and bathrooms, baths, sinks and old loos.

Ronnie Wotton, MDS

Let your eyes be your judge and your pocket be your guide – that's an old Black Country saying. Reclaimed materials are far superior to what's being produced today. The quality's so much better that you can't even draw comparisons. Take bricks. Those made between 1880 and 1900 remain the same quality as when they were first produced; the comparable ones made today are rubbish. Firstly, the old bricks have stood the test of time – there's not a blemish on them. It's the quality of the clay, the way they were fired and produced.

Old Victorian paving stones, too. They're still looking great, but the modern ones, the colour goes in five years, and they tend to crack. Forty years ago I bought 600 old Victorian streetlamps and I sold them all. From then on I had an interest in things made by the Victorians. I've always been interested in why people are throwing away lovely

old items, and destroying wonderful buildings, and they're putting in their places these concrete block buildings which have no architectural value whatsoever. England is full of wonderful buildings. I dislike the waste of throwing away other men's labour, men who took meticulous care in their craftsmanship. That's why I love doing what I do.

I'd say if you are renovating a building, do your best to replace things with materials of the same era. But beware of over-emphasizing things. Simple things look more attractive than those that are ornate, over the top. It's a matter of creating the right balance, and until you understand the balance, then you don't understand the work.

Peter Randle, of Ace Reclamation

I built a chalet bungalow-style house entirely from reclaimed materials I'd acquired through my business. The top floor is made from beautiful maple strip flooring belonging to the dance hall of a demolished local hotel – my wife and I remembered dancing on that same surface years ago. And I've used beams from a barn near a local spot called Hangman's Post – the only red signpost in England, so coloured because of the nearby gallows where Judge Jeffreys sent people to hang! We used 58,000 reclaimed bricks, 15 tons of second-hand timber and 2,500 old clay tiles.

Neville Griffiths, Rococo

For me, the excitement is in the things that have time implanted in them – that's what you can't reproduce, especially things that are slightly bashed about, but with that glorious tinge of age. I hold very strong views about ecological waste, but there are also other worrying factors about the reproduction trade, such as, has child labour been used to reproduce cheap stone products in the third world, and is new timber depleting the rainforests? Do not use reclaimed materials for your home to try and recreate a 'pseudo' style – that will fail. I like things that show age and honesty. Very often you might be offered, say, a fireplace that's got an art nouveau-shaped front with a heavily floral decorated canopy and tiles, and it

Architectural Forum's yard. Although they're based in a shop in a North London street, they've got plenty of room to stock anything and everything. And they do! (Courtesy Architectural Forum)

just doesn't work. For a period house you're going to want to use a second-hand item as the missing link in your architectural jigsaw, so it's got to be just right. Original features in a house make it easier to sell.

Drew Pritchard, of Drew Pritchard

Salvage is ever changing – new types are always coming on stream. The salvage business has morphed hugely, and I would say it is one of the first and best examples of using the internet as a sales tool. It encapsulates the most interesting, exciting and fun elements of the antiques world, and what I find so interesting is to find items that are just so good. I've got items made by craftsmen and artists who were right at the top of their profession – such as William Morris. Not many art galleries can claim to have works by major artists, but quite a few of us salvage dealers have the equivalent of the odd Mona Lisa tucked away.

LASSCO's welcoming Three Pigeons yard. The shop is packed with astonishingly beautiful antique items, there's a quaint coffee shop, and in the farm-sized yard are any number of incredibly huge, rare and astonishing items that you'll long to own. (Courtesy LASSCO Ltd)

CHAPTER 2

Bricks, Roof Tiles and Slates

BRICKS

When matching bricks, size, colour, texture and durability are the key considerations. For matching it's best to take a sample to the architectural salvage yard. Specialist suppliers often offer a matching service, and may be happy for you to email a photo for preliminary enquiries; however, don't make a final decision until you've seen them yourself. Prior to the early nineteenth century, after which railway travel permitted countrywide transportation of building materials, local materials were used in construction, meaning that for an early building, a local salvage yard with vernacular bricks is likely to be your best source. Failing that,

yards that specialize in bricks usually stock a wide variety. Good quality second-hand bricks are likely to cost 10–20 per cent more than standard, newly made bricks, and to be about the same price as specialist handmade bricks.

They are priced per thousand, normally supplied packed densely on pallets, sometimes shrink-wrapped in polythene. Some reclaimed brick specialists assess each brick individually, rejecting flawed items and grading the remainder as to quality. Buying graded bricks guarantees the product, but these are considerably more expensive than ungraded examples. Some yards include half-bricks in the pallet, as these are often needed.

Architectural Salvage Source sell most things, and are known particularly for their vast stocks of bricks. This is how bricks are stored in bulk: shrink-wrapped in polythene and stacked up high on pallets.
(Courtesy Architectural Salvage Source)

Machine-made bricks were first produced in Victorian times; prior to this they were all 'hand-mades', and of less uniform size and appearance. 'Facing' bricks are designed to present a good appearance, 'commons' are used for general construction where appearance is unimportant, whereas 'engineering' bricks have a dense semi-vitreous body with a guaranteed minimum compressive strength, and are used where resilience is an issue.

Colour

Georgian brick colours were largely greys, browns and yellows, in addition to vernacular shades, such as Staffordshire blues, while yellow was an extremely popular brick colour in London until 1850. Lancashire and Staffordshire bricks were bright red

Particularly thin bricks, the size used in Tudor times, but these are unlikely to be as old as that. (Courtesy Abbots Bridge Home & Garden Renovation Centre)

ABOVE: **Average quality red brick, showing the frog.** (Courtesy Architectural Salvage Source)

BELOW: **A less-than-perfect yellow brick – notice how worn and eroded it is at the arrises. It's fine to buy such a brick for less-than-top-quality work – for instance building a garden wall – but make sure you don't pay over the odds for bricks of this quality.** (Courtesy Architectural Salvage Source)

This brick is only about 2in (5cm) thick.
(Courtesy Abbots Bridge Home & Garden Renovation Centre)

due to the soil's high iron content. South Wales, Surrey and Berkshire clays begat blacker bricks, due to the presence of manganese, and East Anglia, Oxfordshire and Hampshire bricks could be whites and greys, indicating the clay's high lime content and absence of iron. The Victorians often utilized bricks of contrasting colours to create patterns, termed 'diapering'.

Colours throughout the medieval and Tudor periods varied from pale pinks and yellows to deep reds. From medieval times to the early eighteenth century bricks were generally predominantly red, sometimes yellow if lime were present, as well as shades of purple. The brick's position in the kiln

Glossary

arris A brick's edge.

bat Part of a cut brick, prefixed by quarter, half, bevelled or three-quarter.

bed Lower or under surface of a brick.

bed joint Horizontal mortar joint.

character The attractive weathered appearance of an old brick.

closer Quarter bat.

course Continuous layer of bricks between bed joints.

cross joint A vertical mortar joint separating two bricks on the same course.

diapers Patterns formed by bricks of contrasting colours and/or textures to make diamonds, squares and lozenge shapes.

face The surface a brick presents.

frog The shallow depression in a brick's upper surface, created to facilitate better bonding by allowing mortar to spread below the brick's top surface.

gauged work When background areas of brickwork are removed, so as to leave a raised design. Also known as 'cut and rubbed work'. The panel's surface is very smooth with almost invisible joints. Used for fine façades to emphasize details and ornamentation, and also for arches and cornices.

header End face of a brick.

jointing Means treating the mortar that is visible in a particular way during construction, as opposed to pointing, where mortar is added to a raked-back joint after construction is complete.

lap The horizontal distance a brick projects over the vertical joints above or below.

perpend Vertical mortar joint as it appears on the face.

pointing Process of adding mortar to a raked-back joint.

quoin Right-angled corner formed in brickwork.

spalling The fragmentation of a brick surface, due to water entering gaps, then freezing and expanding.

squint When two walls meet at an angle that is not a right angle, usually 45 or 60 degrees.

squint quoin Corner formed in brickwork that is not a right angle (obtuse or acute).

stretcher Side face of a brick.

during the firing process influenced colour, too: those nearest the centre tended to be dark blue or black, contrasting with the lighter orange hue of the remainder.

Size

Bricks have always been roughly hand-sized: 9in (229mm) long by 4–4½in (100–115mm) wide, whilst 1550 bricks were around 2in (51mm) thick, steadily thickening to today's 2⅝in (67mm). Victorian machine-made bricks were of a standard thickness, whereas handmades could vary between 2⅝ to 2⅞in (67 to 73mm). In 1965 BS3921 standardized the size to 8⅝ × 4⅛ × 2⅝in (219 × 105 × 67mm), and later in 1969 to the metric brick, measuring 8½ × 4 × 2½in (215 × 102 × 65mm), which replaced the imperial-sized one.

History

Roman bricks were long and thin (1–1½in/ 25–39mm thick) and resembled tiles; in fact they were called 'tegulae', the Latin for tile. After the departure of the Romans (AD412) brick making declined, and while the Saxons reused plenty of second-hand bricks, they also began brick making; by the thirteenth century, Flemish bricks were being exported to England. Early medieval 'great bricks' (12 × 6 × 2in/305 × 152 × 51mm) were in use, but quite rare. By the mid-1200s a size of 8½ × 4 × 2in (216 × 102 × 51mm) was established.

The way to date bricks isn't so much by size (which varied, and still does vary to some extent) as by texture, because techniques for clay weathering, mixing, moulding and firing pertained to different periods. Early thirteenth-century English bricks were made from riverbank clay or clay from shallow beds, termed 'brickearth', a loam clay found in abundance in part of the Thames Valley and eastern England. From the 1700s this was mixed with various other materials.

Clay was usually dug from within the site itself, stirred and turned to give full exposure to the elements for a while, then put into a shallow pit and trodden down by men or oxen. The clay was then either put into a wooden mould or 'forme' to dry, or 'place bricks' were made by spreading the tempered clay on a base of grass or straw, and then cutting it into brick shapes. These fledgling blocks were fired or burnt in a purpose-built kiln, or put into a mobile 'clamp'.

This was made by laying an outer shell of completed bricks, inside which the unfired bricks were stacked in layers sandwiched between combustible materials (charcoal, wood faggots, turf or heather), then the whole was covered over with finished bricks. Finally the pyre was set alight from the outside and left to burn for weeks. Clamp firing produced a lot of wastage, and these failed bricks were called 'semels', 'samels' or 'peckings'.

Timeline

Mid-1500s	Tudor bricks were of irregular size, requiring thick mortar layers to equalize disparities.
1571	Size was regulated by statute – these so-called 'statute' bricks had to be 9 × 4½ × 2in (229 × 115 × 51mm).
1605	A royal proclamation by James I encouraged the use of brick rather than timber.
1625	Charles I's royal proclamation stated that bricks had to be 9 × 4 × 2¼in (229 × 102 × 57mm).
1666	The Great Fire of London occurred, after which builders were forbidden to build with timber. The development of the horse-drawn pug mill – a device for cutting up and compressing the clay – improved brick production, as did the addition to the clay mix of materials such as sand and lime. More accurate bricks, of varying shapes and textures, became available.
1690	The 'frog' was first developed, initially as a clay-saving ploy, but it transpired that the frog allowed more efficient drying and firing, made the brick lighter, and facilitated an improved mortar grip.
17–18th centuries	Dutch brickmakers influenced trends, and clay was dug from deeper layers, rather than from surface deposits.
1700s	Brick quality improved due to more controllable kilns and more size statutes.
1770s	By now bricks were about 2½in (63mm) thick, ½in (13mm) thicker than those of 1550.
1776	Size was standardized again to 8½ × 4 × 2½in (215 × 102 × 65mm).
1784–1851	The period during which the Brick Tax was payable.
19th century	Size was generally 9 × 4½ × 3in (229 × 115 × 76mm).
1850	Supplies of pure brickearth were becoming exhausted, so chalk and other materials were added to the basic clay mix.
1867	Brick-making machines had been developed, presaging the decline of handmade bricks. Beautiful London yellow 'stock' bricks were being produced.
1870s onwards	The majority of bricks were machine-made, resulting in regularity of colour, texture and size. In addition to machine production, the Victorians were using denser clays and improved kilns, all of which resulted in smoother and more uniform products.
1880s	Steam machines could make 1,000 bricks per hour. Specially shaped bricks, such as bullnose and splays, were produced.
1881	A promising belt of clay was discovered at Fletton near Peterborough, and this had many advantages over other clays; the mass-produced 'Fletton' brick soon became popular, and it was reasonably priced.
1965	BS3921 standardized brick size to 8⅝ × 4⅛ × 2⅝in (219 × 105 × 67mm).
1969	Arrival of the metric brick, which was 8½ × 4 × 2½in (215 × 102 × 65mm), replacing the imperial-sized brick.

Types of Brick

Commons Those used for general construction, where appearance is unimportant.

Engineering Having a dense, semi-vitreous body, guaranteeing a minimum compressive strength.

Facing Designed to present a good appearance, available in various colours and textures.

Flettons Originally made from the seam of clay at Fletton near Peterborough, distinctive and very popular, and used throughout the country.

Genuine handmades Hand-thrown, usually with a distinctive creased texture and of irregular shape and size.

Machine-moulded handmade As genuine handmade, but the creased texture is usually less distinct.

Pressed Of regular shape and size, with clean, sharp arrises.

Rubbers, rubbing bricks Especially soft, low-fired bricks for use in gauged work.

Stocks Soft appearance, slightly irregular shape and hand-moulded.

Specials Made in a variety of different shapes and sizes to form angles, corners, plinths, cornices.

Waterstruck Solid, with no holes or frogs and a smooth edge.

Wirecut Made by extruding clay through a dye and cutting off each brick with a series of wires. Featuring sharp arrises with no frogs.

Voussoir Tapering brick, accurately cut for making arches.

Pointing

Double struck Formed like a V coming forwards – popular in Tudor times.

Flush The natural joint is level with bricks or sloping slightly.

Pencilled joints Walls were completely colour-washed, then a pencil brush used to pick out joints in white or black, with whiting and glue size. Not used after early 1600s.

Penny round Ruled with a coin's edge to make a scored recession.

Raked Raked back from the surface, normally used for modern buildings.

Ruled joint A thin groove cut into the joint to create a grid of lines to achieve the illusion of perfect regularity. Popular from the seventeenth to the early twentieth century.

Struck pointing Flush with the lower brick, angled backwards at the top.

Tuck pointing Also known as 'bastard tuck'. Joints were coloured to match the bricks and the building was colour-washed. Then a thin ribbon of lime putty/silver sand was applied into a thin, previously scored line, and trimmed to look like gauged brickwork. Usual from the end of the seventeenth century and continuing until the early 1900s.

Weather-struck and cut The pointing was trimmed off at the bottom. Typically black coloured with red bricks. Predominantly used in the Victorian era, and unsuitable for pre-1850 buildings.

In the mid-fifteenth century bricks were first used *en masse*, notably at Hampton Court (1515), then the largest brick-building enterprise in the country. Fifty years before this time commercial yards with permanent kilns had been established. Medieval bricks were made of pure clay, to which sand was sometimes added. Slip moulding was the method developed to produce the blocks: clay was thrown into an open wooden mould on a bench, and the excess smoothed off, using a wooden stick called a 'strike'. The mould was then removed and the brick placed on a pallet for initial air drying until it acquired a leathery outer coating (which became the weather-resisting 'fireskin'), after which it was fired in the kiln. Brickmakers operated as small independent units, many of them amalgamating into the London Brick Company. Today this company is the only manufacturer of the famous 'Fletton' bricks (*see below*, 'Timeline' 1881, and 'Types of Brick').

Buying Tips/Checkpoints

- Make sure the brick is not crumbly or friable – this indicates that the waterproof 'fireskin' outer surface has become compromised, allowing moisture into the heart of the brick, causing cracking (spalling).
- Reject any brick with thread-like white spores, as this could indicate dry rot infection. While rots cannot damage masonry and only feed off timber, the spores can live in brickwork and be transported to infect areas where there is nearby timber.
- As far as is practical, try to ensure that each brick has one good face and one good end (checking them individually is clearly not an option, since they're packed tightly together).
- Ask to see bricks in the centre of the pallet before buying a large amount – inferior bricks are sometimes 'hidden' away from the edges.
- If they're to be used outside, ask if they've been tested for frost resistance.
- Ideally, buy bricks that have been graded for quality; however, these are more expensive.

Practicalities

You will not find an old, weathered brick with a perfect face or end because it is the weathering that gives it character; in fact a perfectly symmetrical brick with a perfect appearance will always stand out. It is the ageing and weathering in a reclaimed brick that is natural, and impossible to replicate in a manufactured one.

In yards that specialize in second-hand bricks they are often cleaned, then graded and put into 500-brick pallets and shrink-wrapped in polythene. Typically they might be graded into three categories: grade one has a very good face and end, so is the most expensive; grade twos have one or two chips here and there; and for garden walling, for example, grade three would be adequate, as chips and marks look in keeping. Cleaning old bricks is sometimes problematic – the lime-based mortared ones are the easiest to deal with.

Replacing Damaged Brickwork
If your wall is damaged or cracked you can replace an entire brick, turn it back-to-front, or trim it back an inch to insert a 'brick slip' – a specially made 1in (25mm)-thick brick that matches the rest. Replace a single brick by first removing the surrounding mortar: do this by drilling a series of

An opened pack of bricks – check in the middle of packs if you can, since inferior ones are often hidden in the middle of batches like this.
(Courtesy Abbots Bridge Home & Garden Renovation Centre)

holes, or cutting with a hacksaw blade or angle grinder (take care not to damage adjacent brick surfaces). Then cut the old brick away using a pugging chisel. The cavity should be brushed and dampened before mortaring in the replacement, using matching mortar for the pointing.

'Stitch and grout' is a method of reinforcing a stressed area, whilst simultaneously replacing fractured bricks, for instance when a crack extends up a chimney stack. Remove the affected bricks, no more than a metre at a time, then insert reinforcement such as pre-cast concrete lengths or stainless-steel mesh set into adjacent mortar courses. Then insert the replacement bricks.

Mortars

Traditionally, mortar was a levelling agent, required to compensate for bricks that weren't of regular thickness; this was particularly noticeable in the days when the thickness of handmade bricks varied considerably. Now that bricks are of regular thickness, the mortar in modern walls is used more as a glue, and the beds are thin and of regular width.

You need to match the rest of the mortar joints, for which the correct mortar mix is essential. Mortar is a combination of sand with a binding agent, so firstly the sand must be the right colour, and present in the correct proportion. For most constructions built after 1850 the binding agent is cement, which produces a hard, impervious, water-repellent mortar, so that walls acted as a raincoat, excluding dampness. Prior to this time (approximately – cement was invented in 1824), the sand's binding agent was lime, and buildings constructed using these lime-based mortars were constructed in a totally different way, in that the walls were designed to absorb moisture and relinquish it to the atmosphere, like an overcoat. It is vital that any mortar used for repairs must match the remainder: repairs where cement-based mortars are used in lime-mortared walls result in catastrophe. If in doubt, scratch the mortar's surface with a fingernail: lime mortar is soft and friable, whereas cement-based mortar is rock hard.

For the colour of the mortar to match, you need to know the type of sand used and its proportion in the mix, the latter also being responsible for the relative hardness/softness of the result. You can send a sample of your building's mortar to experts (e.g. Anglia Lime), who can scientifically analyse the sample and tell you what type of sand to use and in what proportion. Generally, the com-ponents of lime-based mortars are harder to analyse than those of cement-based mixes. Typical mortar mixes are usually approximately 1:3, binding agent to sand. Sometimes two types of sand were used.

How to Point

Scrape back joints to 1in (25mm) depth, brush them clean, then spray the surrounding wall and crevices with water. When mixing the mortar take care not to add too much water, as a sloppy mortar will splurge out and stain adjacent brickwork. Apply matching mortar with a small trowel or similar tool. Allow the work to partially dry before fashioning the surface to match the remainder. Stipple the finish with a stiff brush after the initial set.

Expert Advice

Peter Minter, of Bulmer Brickwork, makers of bespoke bricks

The problem with buying second-hand bricks is that you seldom get the genuine thing – you may get an old brick, but not necessarily the one that comes from the right geographical area. What we're doing is matching the size and textures to the original to a high degree of accuracy. It's rather like a piece of furniture: you can't just add on 200 years of patina, it's the grime and the polish that give the lustre, and it's the same with bricks. There's an awful lot of ignorance about mortar. Use the wrong mortar, and the brick will never look right. If it's practical, a good plan is to mix bricks from a palette before you lay them, so you've got a range of colours. This will give you a nice composite effect, breaking up the overall colour.

Martin Jump, Northern Sales Director for Blockleys Brick Ltd

Buy from somewhere reputable, as the bricks will have been sorted, cleaned and expertly assessed already, so you'll not be in for any nasty surprises hidden away in the centre of a pallet. Consider the quality of the cleaning and the bricks' general condition. Dry rot or the erosion of the outer water-repellent fireskin can render a brick crumbly and friable – avoid such bricks.

ROOF TILES

Plain Clay Tiles

These rectangular roofing units are available in more than fifty colours; they weather favourably and mellow with age. The old 'peg' tiles were fixed by oak pegs passing through holes cast in the clay, but after 1836 'nibs' were added. These were projecting ears at top edges, designed so the tile could hook on to a wooden batten nailed to the roof; nibbed tiles were in general use by the late nineteenth century. Nibbed tiles also have nail holes cast into them, and it is usual practice to nail them every fourth row and at eaves and verges.

Second-hand plain clay tiles are about 60 per cent of the price of newly made ones, but ridge tiles cost about the same as new. However, elaborate ridge tiles, such as those featuring dragons, are only available second-hand, or as reproduction pieces, and are considerably more expensive than standard ridge tiles.

Clay tiles can either be 'single camber', having a slight curve along their length, or 'double (or cross) camber', where they are also arched from side to side in order to give the roof a more textured appearance. They are of dense composition so as to discourage water and be resistant to extremes of temperature and the growth of moulds and lichens. Vertical tiling refers to a technique whereby clay tiles are hung vertically on to walls, nailed to timber framing. 'Mathematical' tiles are vertically hung tiles specially made to emulate brick, originally created as a way of avoiding the Brick Tax (see below).

Tiles are made from clay that has been dug, then left to weather for at least twelve months. A clay 'batt' is then placed into a mould, pummelled in by hand, the excess clay wired off (cut with a wire), and a punch is used to form the nib and two nail holes are added along the top edge. The unit is allowed to dry to release excess moisture, then fired in a pre-kiln, and finally in a kiln. Once tiles could be made by machine, this became the standard method of manufacture.

Fixing Clay Tiles

Tiles are usually hung 'double lap', meaning each row of tiles half covers the one beneath and also overlaps the top part of the row below that. Rows

An 'Acme' plain clay roof tile, showing the nibs which hook on to the timber battens. Always make sure nibs haven't been broken off.

(Courtesy Abbots Bridge Home & Garden Renovation Centre)

A batch of 'Acme' clay roofing tiles, one of the most popular makes. Notice the nail holes.

(Courtesy Abbots Bridge Home & Garden Renovation Centre)

are set so that the gaps are staggered, occurring halfway along the width of the ones beneath and above. One-and-a-half width tiles are produced so as to facilitate this, fitted at verges on alternate rows. 'Single lap' fixing is where tiles only overlap one row beneath, and is used for interlocking tiles with waterproof side joints (see below). They were originally bedded in a draughtproofing material such as hay or moss, latterly lime mortar.

Profiled Tiles

An opened pack of profiled (Roman) clay tiles, shrink-wrapped in polythene. (Courtesy Abbots Bridge Home & Garden Renovation Centre)

These give an attractive undulating texture to a roof, and, for the profiles that are still made, the prices are more or less the same as new ones. The varieties are as follows:

Roman tiles: These consist of flat 'under'-tiles, fixed flat, and half-round barrel-shaped ones on top. The majority are tapered from head or tail so they can overlap each other, the narrow width of the one above fitting inside the wider width of the one beneath. Under-tiles are nailed flat on tiling battens or close boarding. Over-tiles are nailed to vertical battens fixed between the rows of tiles, the battens being covered by the over-tile.

Spanish tiles: Also known as 'mission' tiles, these are similar to Roman tiles. The difference is that the under-tile is concave and not tapering, and is a match for the corresponding convex over-tile. Under-tiles are nailed into vertical battens at either side, with over-tiles single nailed to the top of the battens.

Pantiles: These are a simpler variation on the Spanish tile. The trough on the under-tile combines with the curve of the over-tile, producing an S-shaped profile for all. Opposing diagonal corners are cut away so as to allow tiles to fit together in the same plane where head and tail meet between courses. They are fixed to tiling battens with a single nail through the single wide nib at the head.

French tiles: Mostly made of red terracotta, these were widely used in the early twentieth century. They have a corrugated profile and interlock at the sides, top and bottom, hang on their nibs from battens, and are not nailed.

A profiled tile, made to interlock at the sides. (Courtesy Abbots Bridge Home & Garden Renovation Centre)

Concrete tiles: A relatively modern invention, these are thicker and heavier than clay or slate, and should not be used to replace either of these, because their weight is likely to damage the underlying structure, which was designed for lighter coverings.

Glossary

accessories Items made of clay or other materials and used in combination with tiles to fulfil a roof's practical requirement, an example being ventilation tiles. The term would also describe cresting.

bonnet tiles Shaped tiles for covering the hips or ridges of roofs.

cresting A feature of some Victorian houses, whereby ridge tiles incorporate a shaped design above, to create a decorative line along the roof's apex.

eave The bottom edge of a roof.

feature tiles Decorative tiles made in special shapes, such as those used in Victorian roofs, often of contrasting colours. Types are named step, pointed/diamond/arrowhead, club, bullnose/beavertail/spade, fishtail. Different designs are usually fitted in alternating rows.

fittings Specially shaped clay roof tiles made to address a particular roofing situation. Examples are valley tile (concave to fit a roof's valley), mansard tile (angled in two directions to suit the angle of a mansard roof), plus four types of ridge tile, made to cover the juxtaposition of two roofing planes at their apex: half-round ridge, third-round ridge, angled ridge and hogsback ridge.

lap Overlap.

man-made slate Originally made from asbestos cement, now produced from fibre cement or concrete mixes.

plain tiles Ordinary rectangular tiles measuring 10½ × 6½in (265 × 165mm).

randoms Slates of random widths, between 11¾–23⅝in (300–600mm) in length.

ridge The line along the roof's topmost angle, where the two planes meet lengthways.

ridge tile (*see* '**fitting**') Half-round or right-angled tile that sits on a roof's ridge, bridging the tiles on both planes.

shaling, splintering, shattering The delaminating of tiles or slates, usually as a result of frost damage.

soakers/eaves course tiles Short tiles, nailed along the eaves before fixing the bottom row of roof tiles, that form an under layer for this first row, thus creating a double thickness of tile at the eaves above the gutter.

tile-and-a-half/gable/verge tile Refers to tiles that are one-and-a-half times the width of standard ones, used on alternate rows at the eaves to facilitate the joints on a row occurring halfway along the tile on the rows below and above.

tingle Flat metal 'hook' used to support a single slate or tile, a device allowing you to install individual units without dismantling the roof above.

tops tile Used at the top of the roof, directly below the ridge, and slightly shorter than plain tiles, measuring 7⅝–8½ × 6½in (195–215 × 165mm).

verge The side edge of a roof.

History

The Romans were the first to use and make fired clay tiles in England, but the practice died out when they left. In 1212 King John issued by-laws for London, requiring combustible roof coverings to be replaced with clay tiles, and from this time onwards roofing tiles were used as a more robust and fire-resistant alternative to thatch. Such was the fear of fire that the use of plain tiles became widespread, so that by the eighteenth century a third of England's houses had tiled roofs.

Size regulation began in 1477–8 during Edward IV's reign, when plain tiles had to be 10½in (267mm) long by 6¼in (159mm) wide (today most are 10½ × 6½in / 267 × 165mm). However, because the manufacturing process was crude, it was not always possible to adhere to the statutory size. Tiles were manufactured alongside bricks, and were often dug from the site where the building was being erected. They were handmade until the arrival of tile-making machines in the 1800s. From 1784–1833 the levy of the Brick Tax led to a burgeoning production of 'mathematical' tiles that mimicked brickwork; a major source of these was a tile works in Staffordshire.

Vernacular differences around the country were

ABOVE: **Profiled tile, possibly one of the many types of pantile.** (Courtesy Abbots Bridge Home & Garden Renovation Centre)

TOP RIGHT: **Different type of clay ridge tile for an acute angled ridge.** (Courtesy Abbots Bridge Home & Garden Renovation Centre)

RIGHT: **Half-round ridge tile; these tiles can also be used on mansard roofs.** (Courtesy Abbots Bridge Home & Garden Renovation Centre)

due to the features of local clay. Clay tiles were made all over Britain where clay was available; the strongest were thought to be those made in the Midlands, from Etruria Marl, while those made in North Staffordshire had a more sophisticated production process, making them more expensive than most. It was discovered that the addition of coloured sand during production could redden the surface. In Shropshire, South Staffordshire and the West Midlands tiles were arranged in the kiln so as to streamline the control of heat that reacted with the iron in the clay, which produced a variety of natural brindle clay colours on the surface.

Interlocking tiles were invented by the Gilardoni brothers in 1841, in Altkirch in the Haut-Rhin. They were made by machine and had interlocking lugs. Then in 1848 Lartigue and Dumas invented the Roman tile. These were large, but in 1875 Royaux and Beghin created the first interlocking small tile. Pantiles were imported from the Netherlands in the early seventeenth century.

Buying Tips/Checkpoints

- Look at the entire stock of tiles you're buying, not just random samples.
- Hip and ridge tiles are rarely available in sufficient quantities second-hand – the only practical solution is to buy these new to match the older second-hand tiles you choose.
- Check for tiles that have broken corners (termed 'shouldered') or missing nibs.
- Make sure they are not delaminated – look carefully at edges, where this phenomenon is evident as the material splitting into friable layers.
- Look out for frost or moss damage.
- Reject any that have adhering urethane foam or black bitumen from previous roof repairs, as neither of these materials can be removed.

ABOVE: **'Dragon' design ridge tile, complete with tail! This 'dragon' style is a favourite for modern reproductions, which can look just as good as the originals.** (Courtesy Cox's Architectural Salvage Yard)

BELOW: **Ridge tile with very attractive cresting.** (Courtesy Abbots Bridge Home & Garden Renovation Centre)

Replacing Clay Tiles

To remove the broken tile, slide a bricklayer's trowel beneath it, then lift the tile with this so that the nibs clear the roof batten, permitting it to slide out from below. If it also happens to be nailed you might be able to lever up the nails using the trowel; alternatively you can use a slate ripper. This is a flat tool whose blade has a small notch in its side at the top, so that by sliding it sideways under the tile this can catch the nail's shaft, allowing you to wrench the nail out by hammering the tool forwards, thereby releasing the tile. To insert the replacement, raise the tiles above using the trowel and slide the newcomer underneath until you feel the nibs slip over the timber batten. If your replacement has no nibs, you need to make a 'tingle': nail a 1in (25mm) strip of sheet lead, copper or zinc, on to the batten, making a turn-up at the bottom at the level of the base of the new tile, and use this to support it.

To fit (or refit) ridge tiles, you need to remove all the old mortar from the underside of the ridge tile and the top of the tiles beneath, then lay a new bed of mortar, using cement and sharp sand mixed in a ratio of 1:3 – you may need to add pigment to colour the mortar. When grouting between the gaps take care not to spread mortar over the tile surfaces as it will discolour them.

Ridge tile incorporating an interesting sculptural shape, the kind normally used at the front of the house. (Courtesy Abbots Bridge Home & Garden Renovation Centre)

Rules for Working on Roofs

Safety:

- In an industrial situation, when people are employed, it is illegal to work above a certain height without using scaffolding; however, this does not apply to homeowners working on their own property. On the other hand, if you are doing much work on a roof it is certainly advisable to use scaffolding, and you should always get professional advice from a health and safety professional on all aspects of safety, such as wearing a hard hat, safety equipment and so on.
- Working at heights is *always* potentially hazardous. You should only do so if you have experience or *full knowledge of all the relevant safety issues and the precautions needed.*
- Never take chances. If you have an aversion to heights it is not worth trying to conquer it – get someone else to do the work for you.
- Don't walk on a roof's surface of tiles or slates as you are likely to slip and/or break them. Hire a specially designed roof ladder that hooks over the ridge, and cushion its feet so it doesn't damage the roof where it rests.

General:

- Don't add felt beneath tiles if there was none there previously. Conversely, if originally there was roofing felt present, you must replace it. Repairing an old building should be a matter of understanding its original construction and putting things back as they were.
- Don't replace tiles or slates with a heavier material, for instance concrete tiles. The supportive structure may collapse or buckle under the extra weight; this is a common cause of roof failure, and the damage can be catastrophic.
- Don't alter or replace any parts of a listed building without obtaining Listed Building Consent.
- Never apply cement grouting to gaps between tiles or slates, except in the case of ridge tiles, which do require grouting.
- Always use roofing nails made of aluminium alloy or copper to re-fix slates or tiles.
- Ensure good ventilation to all roof timbers, possibly by adding vents if required.
- Don't water-blast tiles or slates to clean them, as you will remove their surface patina.

SLATES

These are made from splittable stone and dressed to the correct thickness and size. There are basically two types of genuine slate: thin natural slate, split and dressed to uniform sizes; or thicker, heavier 'stone slate' made from limestone or sandstone and which comes in random sizes. Modern man-made tiles were originally made from asbestos cement, but are now produced using fibre cement or concrete mixes. Key categories of British slate are:

- Bangor or Porthmadoc slates – thin, and blue, purple or greenish grey in colour
- Westmorland slates – thicker, and green or dark blue
- Cornish/South Wales slates – blue-grey to brown

Second-hand slates are around the same price as new ones.

Slates are produced by quarrying the rock, cutting blocks to size, then splitting them as thinly as is practical: too thin and the slates won't be strong enough, too thick is wasteful. Inherently weaker rocks are split to $\frac{3}{8}-\frac{1}{2}$in (8–12mm) thick, while the strongest can be as thin as $\frac{3}{16}$in (4mm) – in fact a thin slate made from strong rock will be as strong as, or stronger than, a thick slate made from weak rock. The edges are then trimmed square and bevelled with a hammer (edge trimming ensures that water drains away from slates). This process was originally done by hand, whereas now it is mostly performed by machine. The nail holes at the centre are punched from the underside, which naturally forms a countersunk hole on the top side, which is ideal for accepting the nail head.

A pallet of slates, showing how thin they are.
(Courtesy Abbots Bridge Home & Garden Renovation Centre)

See how water runs off the tile, which dries almost immediately. (Courtesy Abbots Bridge Home & Garden Renovation Centre)

Slate's natural surface texture varies from smooth to riven, and their colours can be greens, blues, greys, purples and reds, in addition to variegated shades, with stripes or mottled patterns. Standard sizes are 'smalls', 'doubles', 'ladies', 'countesses' or 'duchesses'. The thinnest are known as 'bests', the thickest 'strongs', with 'mediums' in between these. The thickness can vary within batches.

Slates are nailed, using pre-punched holes positioned halfway along the slate's length, which prevent the slate being lifted by the wind. They were fixed with iron nails that were prone to rust; at its terminal stage, this is termed 'nail sickness' when the roof covering slips as a result of the nails' lack of support. The slates were nailed to vertical counterbattens fixed to horizontal battens, so as to create a space for penetrating moisture to drain away freely.

History

Slate-forming rock was made by heat and pressure acting on underwater clays, or more rarely volcanic ash, over a long period. The effect caused the clay minerals to recrystallize and align themselves with their long axis perpendicular to the direction of pressure, and it is this mineral alignment that imparts the property of 'slatey cleavage', making the rock splittable into strong thin sheets. Slate can contain minerals such as carbonates, metallic sulphides and graphite, which are unstable and reduce the material's durability.

By the nineteenth century slate was widely used because it was cheaper than clay tiles, and the roof pitch could be shallower, creating a saving on materials. The Welsh slate industry reached its height in the 1890s when half a million tons were produced and 17,000 men were directly employed. Different coloured slates were used to create decorative effects. However, subsequently the tables turned when clay tiles became cheaper than slates. Production declined, then the quarries closed.

The earliest slates were hung using wooden pegs, not nails, the idea being that when the timber became wet it would expand and thus consolidate adhesion. Torching – a mixture of lime, sand and hair – was applied to the slates' underside between

Broken slates: once on the roof they'll withstand any amount of weathering, but in handling, their thinness and brittleness means they smash easily. (Courtesy Abbots Bridge Home & Garden Renovation Centre)

Buying Tips/Checkpoints

- Check the area between nail holes, as the slate can be prone to splitting along this nail-line.
- Look for hairline cracks or powdering on the reverse.
- When matching slates at a yard, take several examples to compare colour, size and thickness.
- It is important to obtain slates of the same thickness as the remainder. Units that are too thick means that overlapping courses won't lay flat. For the width, you need to allow ⅛in (3mm) between each vertical joint.

the laths or battens, to help hold the pegs in place and to keep the roof windproof. Slates were always laid in courses diminishing steadily in size from the eaves, to the smallest stones at the ridge.

Replacing Slates

As with clay tiles, first lift the casualty with a trowel to try to dislodge the nails. However, you are likely to need a slate ripper to remove these (see above). Alternatively, slide a hacksaw blade up and cut through the nail shafts with this. You will have to make a tingle to support the replacement (see above), as it is not possible to nail the slate in place without removing those above.

For replacements, always use aluminium alloy or copper roofing nails, ¾ to 1in (20–25mm) longer than the slate's thickness. If you need to trim slates to size, the thinnest can be cut by holding them face down on a straight board with the edge overhanging by the required amount, then using the edge of a bricklayer's trowel to chop off the surplus, using the board's edge as a guide.

EXPERT ADVICE

Gerald Selway, of
Rose Green Reclamation

On clay tiles:

Always take a sample with you to the yard; even a broken one is useful for colour and size matching. Reclaimed clay can 'go biscuit' when the protective surface has become compromised, allowing the ingress of frost, which causes spalling. You can get away with one missing nib, but ideally you need two. As for colour, you can get standard terracotta red ones, but also dun-coloured, or slightly darker examples. People sometimes think this colour is a layer of dirt, but it's not: this darker colour is an intrinsic part of the tile which cannot be removed. Take care never to mix this darker colour with red tiles, as it'll give a displeasing effect. If you're buying ridge tiles you not only need to check their length, but also their pitch (the angle inside), which can be 45 degrees or shallower.

Often people will ring me under the impression that they know what they're describing, for instance asking for a 'triple Roman', when in fact they really want a 'double Roman'. There are forty types of clay tile, including single, double and triple Romans, pantiles, and so on. If you're not a roofer you're unlikely to know all the differences, so always bring a sample for comparison.

On slates:

The best second-hand slates to buy are the Welsh ones. There are imported ones from China and Spain that you should avoid. For one thing these aren't such a good thickness, but their chief fault is that the grain goes the opposite way to British slates, which means they can just split and break in half due to the weight; this is because the weight is continually pulling down on the potentially breakable grain lines. In fact the bottom half of such a slate can drop away after only two years. The original Welsh ones had a vertical grain, meaning that the grain was not being pulled along potential fault

lines by the roof. Slates can go powdery and brittle, so check carefully for this. Check a slate by giving it a tap with your knuckle. If it rings, that's fine, but a dull thud means it's gone past its useful life.

On slates and stone tiles you might have a triple lap, whereas with clay or concrete tiles you've just got a 'water' lap, resulting in a lot less weight over the area. A manufactured tile actually has a water bar down the side, so water cants along the side. In contrast, a slate is just a flat piece of material requiring a triple lap, meaning you've got a slate underneath the joint as well.

Roger Mears, Conservation Architect

One of the beauties of pitched roof construction is that you can generally see where there are failures. What's more, tiles and slates are conveniently small, overlapping units which can be replaced individually.

Julian Owen, Conservation Architect

Julian Owen has written three fascinating, fact-packed books for The Crowood Press; see Useful Contacts.

Older traditional roofs had no underfelt, so were consequently well ventilated, and any penetrating rain or condensation would soon evaporate. That's why you should not add underfelt to such older roofs, unless you add extra ventilation. If older roofs are insulated and roofing felt is added without ventilation, any moisture that condenses in the construction is trapped, resulting inevitably in rot. Either the void above the insulation should be ventilated, or a special breathable sheet should be used in place of traditional felt.

Robert Swingler, of
Swingler and Co.

Older man-made tiles are generally better quality than the newer machine-made variety, which can occasionally laminate (or some say delaminate) — that is, split into layers.

CHAPTER 3

Timber Flooring, Timber Beams

TIMBER FLOORING

Wooden flooring has been used since the Middle Ages, although before the eighteenth century was mainly for upper storeys, ground floors being more usually made of earth, tiles or stone. Before the late 1600s, hardwoods oak and elm were the norm, but by the early 1700s pine from the Baltic and Scandinavia was gradually taking over. For this reason it is often a mistake to sand old timber back to bare wood, as in many cases you will discover that the timber is pale blonde or reddish and knotty, and its perceived 'hardwood' appearance was an illusion, and has been produced by staining (notably in the case of Victorian staircases). In parts of East Anglia in particular (and probably other areas) it's important to be aware that for buildings prior to 1700, if you remove painted materials you might also remove important historic paintwork, so consult your local conservation officer, who may be able to recommend local experts who can advise you.

Second-hand timber flooring is usually preferable to new materials, because the wood is likely to be of higher quality, and fully seasoned. It falls into four categories: pine 'floorboarding' is the most common, and 'strip flooring' is similar, the difference being that the boards are much narrower, and strip flooring comes in a variety of different timbers instead of just pine. The other two types are brick-sized wood-block flooring laid in various patterns, and finally flamboyant 'parquet panels': these are relatively thin, and often have elaborately decorated borders.

A stack of lovely old French oak. (Courtesy Victorian Woodworks Ltd)

Very thin old French oak, about to be bonded to a new softwood backing to make robust boards with a historic timber surface. (Courtesy Victorian Woodworks Ltd)

Thick ancient timber joists, about to be cut longitudinally to make floorboards. (Courtesy Victorian Woodworks Ltd)

Assortment of old floorboards, ready to be cleaned up. (Courtesy Victorian Woodworks Ltd)

RIGHT: **Heavy timber joists.** (Courtesy Victorian Woodworks Ltd)

BELOW: **Timber joists of varying sizes.** (Courtesy Victorian Woodworks Ltd)

Second-hand floorboards cost approximately the same price as new material, whereas second-hand floor joists are around 50 per cent of the price of new timber – but bear in mind that old joists may need to have their nails removed, and must be handled with great care so you are not injured by the protruding nails. Prices for parquet flooring vary so enormously that it is not practical to compare the prices of old and new.

Glossary

beam Large structural timber for supporting floor joists.

boards/floorboards The relatively thin planks of wood nailed to supportive joists, whose top surface is the room's floor.

character grain Timber with lots of knots.

chase A channel cut into a wall for pipes, wiring or joist ends.

corbel Stone or timber wall bracket that supports a structural member.

fillet Wedge of timber for pushing floorboards closer together and filling gaps.

firrings Tapered timbers nailed to the top of level joists to create a slope or to level them up.

joist Heavy timber laid on edge, for supporting floorboards, to which they are nailed.

lintel Timber, metal or concrete member over an opening designed to support the weight above.

secret nailing The practice of inserting small-headed nails at an angle into each floorboard on the tongued side, so that the heads are concealed by the next plank.

sleeper wall A low wall built up from the foundations to support a suspended ground floor.

square-edged Describes the edge of a board, of a type that butts up against its neighbours.

suspended floor Where ground-floor joists are supported so as to hold the floor above an earth or concrete subsurface.

tongue-and-grooved One of the earliest types of 'engineered' methods of jointing timbers side by side. One side of a board has a protruding central 'tongue' of timber along its edge, and a groove along the other, facilitating adjacent boards slotting together along their edges' length. The slot and tongue are normally made non-central in the timber's thickness, so that boards have a top side and bottom side.

wall plate Timber fixed along a wall to provide a fixing for structural members.

ABOVE: **Close-up to show the beautiful tongue-and-groove edging on these old boards.**
(Courtesy Victorian Woodworks Ltd)

ABOVE RIGHT: **Old timber waiting to be processed.** (Courtesy Victorian Woodworks Ltd)

BELOW RIGHT: **Timber that has recently been saved from an ancient building.**
(Courtesy Victorian Woodworks Ltd)

Just some of Victorian Woodworks' vast stocks of second-hand timber. (Courtesy Victorian Woodworks Ltd)

Floorboards

Joists normally run from front to back, or side to side, of a house and are laid equidistantly, and floorboards are nailed across them at right angles. Joists on the ground floor usually rest on sleeper walls, or sometimes have several bricks supporting them at each end and at points along their length, so the floor is suspended above the earth – a suspended floor. Occasionally, in cheaply built houses, the joists may be placed directly on to the earth, and will quickly rot away. For first and higher floors, joists are built into the wall at each end, but because this timber is imprisoned in damp masonry, this practice often leads to the timber rotting away. Sometimes a number of joists might rest on a supportive, much larger beam, which in turn is held up by masonry.

If you have damaged supportive joists, on the whole it is best to replace these with new timber that has been assessed for its structural strength; and if you've had rot or infestations, it is often wisest to buy this wood pressure-treated with preservative.

Second-hand floorboards will nearly always be of pine, unless the material is particularly old and valuable; they may possibly be of oak, although for ordinary houses, oak hasn't generally been used for flooring since the 1700s. Sizes can vary as to width:

from 4–8in (102–203mm) is usual (the older the wider), and ¾in (20mm) in thickness. Four distinct varieties of pine were used between 1830 and 1930, all of which have characteristic colours. These are Colombian (yellow/pink), Baltic (yellow), Douglas fir/Oregon (clear pink) and pitch pine (red). If you are replacing boards and propose the boards to be seen, you'll need to take a sample that you've sanded back to bare wood so as to compare the colour.

A stack of floor joists with the nails still protruding – take great care when handling and transporting these, as the nail heads can be as sharp as a razor and can easily tear your skin. (Courtesy Cox's Architectural Salvage Yard)

More of Victorian Woodworks' vast stocks of
timber. (Courtesy Victorian Woodworks Ltd)

Parquet Panels

Parquet panels are usually 11sq ft (1sq m) or smaller, made up of pieces of thin timber (¼–⅜in/6–10mm), and are sometimes surrounded by decorative border strips. These panels are typically made into prearranged patterns with names such as 'Parquet de Chantilly' or 'Parquet de Versailles'. They are pinned and glued to the wood subsurface beneath. They can be extremely dramatic and impressive, and are also relatively expensive, whether made from new or reclaimed timber.

Strip Flooring

This is so named because, while it is similar to floorboards, it tends to be much narrower; it is usually tongue-and-grooved, and was produced from a variety of different timbers, amongst which are eucalyptus woods, cherry, walnut and bamboo. Used in Georgian times, but particularly popular in the 1920s, this tongue-and-grooved type of board is narrower than standard floorboards, being up to 4¼in (110mm) wide and ¾in (20mm) thick. Strip flooring can look very impressive in a period home, and can overlay a standard floor-boarded area or be fixed direct to joists.

ABOVE: **Craftsmen laying out the reclaimed and machined old timber pieces to assemble a parquet panel. Each panel is made by hand from genuine old timber.** (Courtesy Victorian Woodworks Ltd)

BELOW: **The parquet pieces, precision cut to size, about to be assembled.** (Courtesy Victorian Woodworks Ltd)

A made-up parquet panel: 'Parquet de Versailles Panels Massif'. (Courtesy Victorian Woodworks Ltd)

ABOVE: **A craftsman applying wood dye to an assembled parquet panel.** (Courtesy Victorian Woodworks Ltd)

TOP LEFT: **A finished parquet panel 'Parquet de Chantilly Panels Massif' – just look at the textures and contours of the beautiful timber.** (Courtesy Victorian Woodworks Ltd)

LEFT: **A completed parquet panel.** (Courtesy Victorian Woodworks Ltd)

Woodblock Flooring

Woodblock flooring is sometimes confused with parquet, whereas woodblock is exactly that: tongue-and-grooved or plain-edged blocks about 2¼–3in (57–75mm) wide, 9–12in (225–305mm) long and around ¾in (20mm) thick. Sometimes their edges are joined by pegs or dowels, inserted into holes in each. The blocks are made from exotic hardwood timbers such as Burmese teak, obeche and jarra. Originally they were arranged into a layer of 'black jack', a bituminous tar laid on the subfloor. This material is virtually impossible to remove without machinery, so when you buy second-hand woodblocks, ensure that this bituminous tar has been removed, and the blocks machined to a uniform thickness. Nowadays standard practice is to use a gap-filling adhesive to fix them. They can be laid in various patterns, including square brick, diagonal brick, herringbone, square basket and diagonal basket. If a woodblock floor is damaged it may be possible to make patch repairs by cutting out sections and replacing them.

Modern Floors

Don't confuse old timbers with modern timber floor finishes, which are basically either solid wood boards (the most expensive) or various 'engineered' timbers. These are: 'multilayer' – a layer of hardwood fixed to a sandwich of softwood boards; 'veneer' – a very thin layer of surface hardwood bonded to softwood; or, cheapest of all, 'laminate' made from plastic laminate printed with a wood pattern and bonded to a fibreboard base.

New Boards Made from Old

Companies such as Victorian Woodworks Ltd produce new flooring materials made from gen-

Old woodblock flooring. These blocks are dirty and are not of uniform thickness because of the bitumen fixing on the back that still adheres – they are about to be cleaned up and machined to a uniform thickness. (Courtesy Victorian Woodworks Ltd)

BELOW: **Woodblock flooring. As in the previous photograph, these blocks are as they were removed from a building, prior to cleaning and machining; if you tried to lay them as they are, your floor would be a disaster. The protruding pegs engage in corresponding holes.** (Courtesy Victorian Woodworks Ltd)

MIDDLE RIGHT: **The top surface of old woodblocks, scuffed and scratched. Once they are cleaned up they'll look as good as they did a century ago!** (Courtesy Victorian Woodworks Ltd)

BOTTOM RIGHT: **Woodblocks and old timber boards.** (Courtesy Victorian Woodworks Ltd)

uine old timber boards. One example is their engineered flooring, whereby a new softwood backing is bonded on to thin old timber planks, thereby permitting the convenience of modern 'engineered' floor laying with the beauty and grandeur of ancient timber. Another example of their products is beautiful parquet panel flooring made using ancient timbers and assembled by craftsmen. They also rejuvenate old woodblock flooring by machining the blocks down to a uniform size, and cleaning the tongue-and-grooved edges to facilitate easy assembly.

ABOVE: **Close-up to show how Victorian Woodworks make engineered flooring by bonding historic timber on to new softwood backing boards, whose profiled edges lock together.** (Courtesy Victorian Woodworks Ltd)

LEFT: **Floorboards machined to uniform size.** (Courtesy Victorian Woodworks Ltd)

BELOW: **Old timber boards bonded to a softwood backing with no profiled edges, intended for butting up against each other.** (Courtesy Victorian Woodworks Ltd)

Timeline

Medieval	Floors were mainly made of oak, occasionally elm, of boards up to 450mm (18in) wide. Originally boards were laid parallel to flat joists which were rebated to accept them, the joist's central section itself forming part of the floor's surface. Traditionally boards were lap-jointed, meaning that their thickness was halved to facilitate them fitting together to form a uniform surface.
Pre-1600	Joists were still being laid flat instead of on edge, as it wasn't realized that more supportive strength was achievable by laying them on edge, as has been the practice since this was discovered in many parts of the country, but not, however, everywhere.
1600s	Timbers of choice were still oak, elm or other hardwoods, board width being 12in (305mm). Joists began to be laid on edge, but even long after this date, especially in East Anglia, joists were still laid flat.
Early 1700s	From this time onwards pine, imported from the Baltic and Scandinavia, was used and began gradually to replace the dwindling supply of home-grown hardwoods. These boards were of random widths and were often painted to resemble the more expensive hardwoods, or sometimes finished in a plain colour, then decorated with a stencil or freehand graining design.
1800s	By now pine had replaced oak as the floor timber of choice. Boards were of more regular sizes, as a result of the nineteenth century's increasing mechanization.
1820s	Tongue-and-grooved boards were first created: before this, boards simply butted up against each other. Parquetry was first invented, but was not in common use.
1880	Tongue-and-grooved flooring had become ubiquitous.
1900–1910	Parquetry flooring was growing in popularity, especially in more affluent homes.

Very old elm boards. Most elm of this age has long since succumbed to decay.
(Courtesy Victorian Woodworks Ltd)

Floorboards stacked floor-to-ceiling, plus some woodblocks. (Courtesy Victorian Woodworks Ltd)

Buying Tips/Checkpoints

- **Moisture content:** Buy from a dealer who has stored the timber properly. If stored outside the timber may absorb moisture, meaning that it will shrink and crack in a centrally heated home. The moisture content should be 9–11 per cent. Alternatively you can buy wet timber, but store it loose in your home for nine months before laying it, so it can dry out. Moisture content can be detected by using a moisture meter.
- **Infestation:** Check for woodworm – common furniture beetle – infestation (1/32in/1mm holes coupled with fresh dust), or larger holes which can indicate deathwatch beetle, or other pests.
- **Rot:** Wet rots are black or brown, leaving spongy areas with horizontal and cross-grain cracks, and may have thread-like strands. The more serious dry rot (avoid anything contaminated with this at all costs) is evident as cracks across the grain, and cuboid cracking, light grey strands with white growths or grey sheets with patches of yellow or violet, and has coloured fruiting bodies. Examine the timber's underside, where the grain is open and unsealed. White deposits on old timber, especially floorboards, can often be merely a deposit of dried plaster or cement.
- **Warping:** Look along the length of the timber for evidence of this. However, a slight degree of warping is inevitable and usually unavoidable.
- **Non-aligned tongue-and-groove:** These elements of the board may have worn down over time, and are therefore not matching, which would produce an uneven floor surface. In addition, boards may be mixed from different sources, meaning the position of the tongue-and-groove does not match.
- **Clogged grooves in tongue-and-groove:** Particularly for woodblock, when the grooves could be clogged with tar.
- **Woodblock edges, grooves and thickness:** The underside of woodblock flooring may still have a thickness of black jack (the original fixing material) adhering, meaning that the blocks will be of different thicknesses. Make sure your supplier has machined off this tar-like material so all the blocks are the same thickness.
- **Woodblock sizes:** Check that lengths and widths within the batch are identical.
- **Timber colour:** Four distinct types of pine were used (*see* above), so if you are matching floorboards in your home, take a sample that you've sanded down to bare wood, so you can compare its colour with that of the timber you propose to buy.

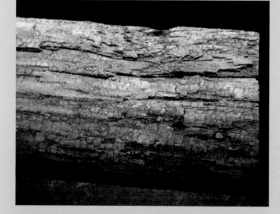

Close-up to show apparent decay. These friable damaged areas are removed, and the board is machined back to solid timber.

(Courtesy Victorian Woodworks Ltd)

Cracks and old woodworm holes add to the charm and beauty of this ancient timber.

(Courtesy Victorian Woodworks Ltd)

Close-up to show woodworm holes. No worm is active here, because Victorian Woodworks' heating process kills them. However, avoid any timber with woodworm that you find in conventional salvage yards, as it is unlikely to have been treated, and the worm may still be active. (Courtesy Victorian Woodworks Ltd)

ABOVE: **Close-up of cracked timber, the kind of flaw which adds to its charm.** (Courtesy Victorian Woodworks Ltd)

BELOW: **Woodworm damage at a joist end.** (Courtesy Victorian Woodworks Ltd)

Practicalities

Cleaning

Wax or dirt can be removed using coarse wire-wool soaked in methylated spirits. To take away paint and stains, use a solvent-based stripper or a poultice-type stripper for deep-seated stains. SPAB advises that hardwood floors should only be cleaned infrequently, as pools of water can raise grain and cause warping, rot or expansion; they also advise using cold or warm water with neutral PH soap, which should then be rinsed and mopped dry.

You can also hire a large drum sander for cleaning a complete floor, but these remove a lot of material, so ensure that your floor isn't too thin for this, and be aware that removing the surface layer may reveal an inferior substandard surface. Before using a drum sander it is vital to punch nails well below the timber's surface, otherwise expensive abrasive belts will be instantly destroyed. Never use a drum sander for an old oak floor unless you are certain it has always been free of woodworm: any past woodworm infestations may mean that just below the top surface are a network of 'worm runs' and if these are exposed the floor may be ruined, or you will have to sand down a considerable depth.

Gaps between Floorboards

Small gaps between floorboards are acceptable. For larger gaps, take up and re-lay the boards closer together, filling the final end gap with an extra trimmed-down board. Clean up the edges of the boards individually with sandpaper before re-laying them. One way of cramping the boards tightly together as you lay them is to hammer large nails into the joists in front of the new board, then pack wedged timber packers between the board's edge and these nails prior to nailing the board to the joists. If the gaps aren't too big, forget about it – a slight gap in a floor is in keeping with how it should look, and is often due to the introduction of dry central heating.

Squeaky Boards

Squeaks occur either because boards are not

nailed down to joists securely enough, or because they are rubbing against their neighbours, or they have been sanded down too much and are too thin, and therefore cannot support weight adequately. Loose boards are often the result of previous lifting for the installation of services, so there are likely to be cables or pipes beneath, so take great care when fixing them, in case of this. Once you are satisfied you won't puncture a cable or pipe, try screwing the loose boards down rather than nailing: screwing is a less intrusive, safer and more efficient way of fixing timbers than using nails.

Removing/Replacing Boards
If you have a historic home with ancient boards, take special care when removing these, as it is very easy to break them. The SPAB (Society for the Protection of Ancient Buildings: *see* Useful Contacts) information leaflet *Patching Old Floorboards* is extremely informative, as is their technical pamphlet *The Care and Repair of Old Flooring*.

Before starting any repair to a standard floor, make sure there are no electric cables or water or gas pipes beneath where you plan to cut – if there are, take great care. If you have a tongue-and-grooved floor, first cut off the tongues on either side using either a panel saw or floorboard saw, or a circular saw with the cut carefully adjusted so it cuts no deeper than the board's thickness – adjust the depth of cut progressively. Then decide on the position of your widthways cut(s) so that you are directly above the centre of a joist: you may be able to see the joists through gaps between boards; alternatively the position of the nails in the boards is a giveaway. Do this cut by drilling a line of ⅛in (3mm) holes along the line, then use a chisel to complete the cut. Remember, cables and pipes

These holes are later filled, using epoxy resin-based filler. (Courtesy Victorian Woodworks Ltd)

Old woodworm holes filled with epoxy resin-based filler. (Courtesy Victorian Woodworks Ltd)

A finished timber floor, made of ancient wood, showing its beautiful grain and finish.
(Courtesy Victorian Woodworks Ltd)

Stains, Varnish and Wax

Always test the product on an inconspicuous area before applying overall.

Wood stains/dyes: Either white-spirit or water-based. These should be applied rapidly with a large rag. They can only ever darken a timber and will never lighten it.

Varnishes:

Oil-based polyurethane Available in matt, satin or high gloss, these give timber a yellowish tinge and are waterproof.

Water-based acrylics Available in matt, satin and clear gloss, these are quick-drying and odourless, and dry transparent; they are environmentally friendly.

Marine or yacht varnish A high gloss, oil-based varnish that gives a tough finish; special types made for treating floors are available. Apply in several thin coats.

Varnish stains: Predominantly polyurethane-based, these contain stain and varnish; a disadvantage is that if the surface is subsequently chipped, the damage is immediately apparent because the stain disappears from the chipped area along with the finish.

Oils: Only trip-trap oil is suitable for flooring, as it penetrates the grain, hardening it and also forming a protective skin. Oils darken timber, but give it a mellowness.

Waxes:

Beeswax, carnauba and coloured wax are the different varieties available. They give a beautiful sheen to timber and the most attractive long-term finish, and successive layers produce a patina. A disadvantage is that they are hard work to keep up, because they trap dirt and require regular replacement and buffing. For waxing beams, a good method of application is to mix beeswax with turpentine substitute, then paint this solution on the timber's surface, let it dry, then buff it up with a cloth.

often pass through grooves cut in joists, so be particularly careful not to encounter one – use a metal detector, the type used when you are drilling into a wall, to detect the presence of electric cables below the surface.

Carefully lift one end of the board by inserting a 4in (100mm) wide bolster and levering with this, making sure you do not damage adjacent boards. Once the end is free, progressively insert the bolster or a crowbar so as to lift board from each of the joists. Use protective blocks of timber to protect the areas where the tools meet the other boards.

If you're fixing boards to springy joists, use screws instead of nails.

Stacks of finished solid hardwood timber.
(Courtesy Victorian Woodworks Ltd)

ABOVE: The ends of old planks. Timber can look dirty, cracked and discoloured, but the damage is usually only to the top layer. (Courtesy Victorian Woodworks Ltd)

BELOW: End-grain view of stacks of old boards. (Courtesy Victorian Woodworks Ltd)

ABOVE: An assortment of different-sized timbers. (Courtesy Victorian Woodworks Ltd)

BELOW: Old timber joists. (Courtesy Victorian Woodworks Ltd)

EXPERT QUOTES

Declan Molloy, Victorian Woodworks

It's very important to buy woodblock flooring from people who have stored it properly and kept it dry. If they pick up just 1 or 2 per cent moisture, it means that after you've laid them, sanded and sealed them, once your central heating goes on you get shrinkage right across the floor, and it just looks dreadful and there's no way you can repair it.

Secondly, make sure the blocks you buy have had their grooves cleaned and that the tar has been removed and they've been machined to a uniform thickness. The main problems when buying floorboards are matching the colour, getting the right thickness, woodworm, and, as with woodblocks, moisture content. We kiln-dry our timber, which guarantees to kill any worm or larvae, and reduces the moisture content to 9–11 per cent. In the past we've made up one-square-metre parquet panels for very famous people, including pop stars and world class chefs, using 400- and 500-year-old oak.

Roger Mears, architect with Roger Mears Associates

Most second-hand timber available is actually much denser than today's softwood, with a tighter grain, and is much more resistant to decay, which is why it always makes sense to repair an old timber floor or window, preferably with salvaged timber, than replace it with something new. The old timbers were much better, and of course they're fully seasoned and won't warp.

Phil Wilson, Victorian Woodworks

Handmade parquet one-metre-square panels can be made from 300- to 400-year-old timber. They evoke a period of extraordinary splendour, the Versailles ones especially; the Chantilly panels give a more countrified look. We've put a lot of these types of floor into upmarket areas of London, eighteenth- and nineteenth-century houses mostly; they evoke a kind of grandness. As for woodblock, the exotic timbers we have are extraordinary, including jarra, mninga and maple.

Fantastic colours, they go from a nice light oak to almost a blood-red colour, to mahogany or Rhodesian or Burmese teak, a greeny-goldy colour almost. They can go in any period house; designers and architects use them to create effects. The different colours and types of wooden floor can act as a foil to decorative schemes, they can expand and make a room look bigger. You can make a small room look really busy by using a character-grain timber. Reclaimed timber has pinholes, cracks, shakes and splits, which all add to the character and attraction. An attractive charismatic wooden floor can act as a foil in a room, it acts as a focal point, a talking point. One approach is to have a strong floor, treat your curtains as paints, then have light, straightforward decorations, and maybe rugs or a throw.

Philip Poels, of Strippers

To remove a very thick wax layer, first try coarse wirewool and methylated spirits applied with a rag. For sealants or coatings underneath your best bet would be our solvent-based stripper NB510 – this might also remove wax if it's a thin layer. You might get a floor that's been painted around the edge to fill in around a non-fitted carpet. The NB510 might take that off, but if it's penetrated you may need to use a poultice-type alkali-based stripper, Kling Strip, to effectively 'suck' the stain out. Always use Kling Strip for deep-seated stains.

Thornton Kay, Salvo

If you're using second-hand wood flooring with no guaranteed moisture content, then ideally you shouldn't fix it down until it has acclimatized to the humidity of your centrally heated house, which could take a month or three. Wood shrinks a lot across the grain.

TIMBER BEAMS

You can get 400-year-old oak beams, and they'll not only look better than new timber, but they won't warp out of shape, as new 'green' unseasoned wood can. Either beams have been used externally and exposed to the weather, as for building the structures of timber-framed buildings

Old timber beams. Some ends are rotted, but the main sections are all right.
(Courtesy Abbots Bridge Home & Garden Renovation Centre)

Huge old oak beams lying in the yard – these have probably come from a demolished ancient building. (Courtesy Abbots Bridge Home & Garden Renovation Centre)

or barns, or they might have been removed from interiors – for instance you can sometimes find complete assemblies of ceiling timbers. Beams are priced per cubic foot, and are available with cross-sectional sizes varying from around 6 to 14in (152–356mm) square.

The modern equivalent of old oak timber is new 'green' oak, and this material, which will inevitably warp considerably, is frequently used for repairing old timber structures. But since its colour, ageing and appearance is so different, comparing its price with that of old beams is pointless.

In practical terms very old hardwood timber beams are nearly always going to be made of oak. In the past elm, with its beautiful appearance, was popular, but this less substantial timber was more prone to insect attack, so hardly any ancient elm now remains. The two types of oak found in the UK are 'common oak' (*Quercus robus*, *aka* English or pedunculate oak) and 'sessile oak' (*Quercus petraea*). Branches of the sessile oak are straighter than those of the common oak, and the main trunk is less branched. Common oak has stalked acorns, whereas sessile oak has no stalks.

External timbers were treated in different ways according to their geographical location. In the West Midlands, Lancashire and Cheshire timber framing is blackened, giving 'magpie' or black-and-white construction, whereas in eastern counties the timber facing was left natural. In areas where timber-framed buildings were traditional it is a common misconception that limewash was used to cover internal timber beams; in fact it was not used generally, although it might have been applied to obscure earlier paintwork, because it forms a barrier, deliberately used to seal in earlier, perhaps medieval paint layers. Take care if you remove old paint from timber beams, because you may be removing valuable historic old paintwork – always take professional advice. Limewash should definitely not be used to paint internal timber beams.

If you are buying a beam to replace a structural member – for instance one to be used above an inglenook fireplace, or a lintel above a door or window – you have to make sure it has the required strength, so you'll need to consult a structural engineer and/or your local building inspector. If the beam is replacing something similar, fifteenth- and sixteenth-century carpenters tended to use timber that was generally 'over strength', meaning that a like-for-like replacement should be adequate; however, always check with your local building inspector, whose approval you must have, and for a listed building you'll also need listed building consent, and the agreement of your local conservation officer. The usual structural test is to support the beam at each end and put a load in the middle, then measure the deflection: the supportive strength is dependent on this 'deflection factor', rather than whether the beam withstands breakage. If your building inspector, structural engineer or conservation officer says your beam isn't sufficiently strong for its proposed location, a good solution is to use steel structural supports behind it: the timber conceals the metal, and is merely decorative.

Buy from specialist yards, ideally the kind of place that dismantles barns or ancient buildings. As stated earlier, you may be able to buy a complete ceiling assembly, dismantled with instructions for reassembly, and in some cases you can buy a complete dismantled building. Such specialist dealers are likely to have an expert available, who will advise you.

Interestingly, if you examine old beams on ancient buildings, the surface is often eaten away by woodworm; this is usually unimportant, because the rot is normally confined to up to only about half an inch below the surface, leaving the structural heart of the timber unaffected. This attack is caused by woodworm (common furniture beetle), which attacks the outer, softer nutritious sapwood but cannot penetrate oak's rock-like heartwood. And if the timber has lasted three to four hundred years without decaying any further, you can be confident it will last for a long time to come.

Railway sleepers are available, but are obviously of a limited size. Also their use is restricted because they are usually full of all kinds of hazardous, possibly inflammable, chemicals; consequently it's illegal to use them anywhere where they can come into contact with children, for instance in gardens or playgrounds. They have normally been pressure-treated with creosote-type preservatives. If you buy railway sleepers you are usually required to sign a declaration that you won't use them in a garden, playground or anywhere where children might come into contact with the harmful timber. What is more, EU law now forbids the use of creosote-treated timber inside buildings – or indeed anywhere else. However, some kinds of railway sleeper, for instance those from Eastern Europe or made from

Australian redwood, have not been treated with chemicals, and these can be used safely; even so, these 'untreated' timbers are normally destined for landscaping projects rather than for building purposes.

ABOVE: **Assortment of lovely old beams and joists.** (Courtesy Abbots Bridge Home & Garden Renovation Centre)

BELOW: **Close-up of solid oak beams.** (Courtesy MASCo Architectural Salvage Yard)

Glossary

adze A historic tool used to cut or smooth wood. Imagine an axe with the blade turned at right angles, and set with a slight curve to it, like a curved-fingered hand. This tool leaves characteristic marks on the cut surface.

apotropaic marks 'Evil-averting' markings, placed on timber beams in the framer's yard to protect the home against witch's familiars, such as frogs and toads. The practice was popular in the sixteenth and seventeenth centuries, and continued well into the late 1800s.

bressumer Beam at the front of the building.

carpenters' marks A shorthand numbering system, to enable the builder of a timber-framed building to re-erect the structure he has first built in his yard.

chimney beam Also known as a mantle beam, this is the horizontal beam above a fireplace opening, often charred by the fire.

clamp Wedge-shaped timber nailed or pegged to the wall to support ceiling joists.

common joists The thinner beams on a beamed ceiling, jointed at right angles to the central joists (about 4–6in/100–150mm square).

deathwatch beetle Type of serious wood decay where the beetles are deep within the timber and make a characteristic clicking sound; the name originates from the sound heard by bereaved relatives sitting with a corpse in church prior to burial, and hearing the clicking in the rafters overhead. It is difficult to eradicate. Characterized by ⅛in (3mm) diameter holes.

defrassing The removal of timber's surface layer, which has been so degraded by beetle attack that it is no longer structurally useful.

frass The honeycombed or powdered residue of beetle-attacked timber.

green oak 'New' oak timber that has been cut down within a year or so.

heck post/witch post This term is used only in the Lake District and northern areas, and means the post that supports the fireplace beam.

midrail Horizontal timber built into the wall to give bearing support for joists.

pit saw Medieval two-man saw, designed for one person to stand underneath the log, the other above, so they pulled and pushed each end of the saw across the log in unison.

principal joists The thicker beams on beamed ceilings (8–14in/203–356mm square).

scrawkings Colloquial Yorkshire term for carpenters' assembly marks.

ritual deposit A single item of spiritual significance placed under a floor during a building's construction.

side axe Medieval tool for cutting timber.

spiritual midden Chute hidden behind a wall beside a fireplace, open at the top, allowing people to go into the roof space and drop discarded household objects, notably shoes, into the space as a defence against witchcraft and evil. The crucial aspect is that these objects were all worn out, and a family might deposit objects in this way for 200 years.

woodworm The common furniture beetle. Characterized by 1/32in (1mm) diameter holes. If you see the holes in oak, this is likely to signify an attack that's past and now dead.

Ceilings

Beamed ceilings were made by a lattice formed by larger 'principal joists' into which smaller 'common joists' are jointed at right angles, and floorboards for the floor above were nailed on top. Sometimes complete beam assemblies for a ceiling are available. Frequently in cottages, the common joists were concealed, with lath-and-plaster applied to them underneath, leaving the principal beams exposed. Sometimes principal beams were also plastered in more formal houses – you can tell if a beam has been plastered in the past, as it will have many small axe nicks on the surface, which would have been put there originally so as to form a key for the plaster.

It is very important to realize that from the early sixteenth century onwards it was frequently the norm to have flat plaster ceilings either side of the central main beam. Never assume because you have an ancient plaster ceiling that this conceals a network of joists, because this was often not the case. When glass windows were invented this kind of plain white ceiling was deliberately used and painted white in order to maximize the window light.

One method for creating a beamed ceiling is to split beams in half, then stick them to the ceiling with a PVA-based adhesive, and paint around it, so it appears the timber is an intrinsic part of the ceiling. Adhesive alone may be insufficient for support and beams are likely to need additional fixing – if in doubt, check with a structural engineer.

A practical strategy used when installing a complete ceiling/floor system into a house is to effectively fix a 'false ceiling' above the old timbers, to create a cavity for services and insulation materials. You start off with the oak-joisted ceiling framework, then 2 × 4in (51 × 102mm) softwood timbers are nailed (on edge) onto the top side of the principal joists – they are of course narrower than the timbers they're fixed to. Then between these softwood joists you fix plasterboard to the top surface of the principal joists, so from below all you see is the ceiling timbers, with plasterboard in between; previously, this plasterboard has had a couple of coats of plaster applied to it, so isn't a smooth surface. Finally you can put pipes, services and insulation into the 4in (100mm) cavity formed by the softwood joists, then fix floorboards to these, so you have incorporated modern facilities into an attractive historic ceiling/floor assembly.

Witchcraft and Wood Markings

Carpenters' Marks

Frame assemblies for timber-framed buildings were usually made in the carpenter's yard, then disassembled for reassembly on site. Accordingly, 'carpenters' marks' were put on to the individual beams to facilitate reassembly, and the majority of marks you are likely to see will be these. Timber-frame construction expert and master carpenter Wayne Kirby explains:

Carpenters' assembly marks were usually Roman numerals, carved with a rase knife on to the upper face of beams. Each mark gives a number of every member within its frame, and there's another number to identify the frame to which it belonged. 'Levelling marks' indicate points that should align with each other during construction, used during the frame's layout, and 'hewing marks', made by the person who cut the tree into sections, were added when the timber was shaped. Very early marks were more like scratches, whereas in the seventeenth and eighteenth centuries markings were actually chiselled into the surface.

Apotropaic Marks

In the sixteenth and seventeenth centuries when witchcraft and demonology were feared, 'apotropaic marks' were inscribed on timbers (and walls, ironwork, stonework and doors) by builders to ward off witchcraft, evil and ghosts. Openings in the home, such as doorways, windows and fireplaces, were thought to be sites where such entities could enter, so it was at these places that the house had to be protected from witches' familiars, such as frogs and toads. In Suffolk they were frequently used on chimney beams, as they were in Kent, Surrey and Sussex.

To see apotropaic marks, which were often faint, you may need to use torchlight shone crossways at a certain angle. There are two depths of cut, combined together – the deeper ones were made by a carpenter's rase knife, and lighter ones by a scratch awl or knife.

Practicalities

Oak is very hard to cut, and you will quickly blunt saw blades. If you have to use green (new) oak within an assembly – for instance to fill in a missing timber in a construction – remember it's going to warp a lot, over a long period of time – in a year you can easily get ½in (13mm) of shrinkage, as opposed to old timber which will not move as it is fully seasoned, and has about a 10 per cent moisture content.

Cleaning/Removing Surface Finishes

For interior beams you should take care when

removing old paint, as you may be removing very old original and valuable coloured surfaces, which you ought to get advice on, as they may be of historical importance. Prior to 1700 you get red and yellow ochre, and after this date you might find black pigment, or grey – black pigment mixed with whiting. In East Anglia, all interior timbers were painted from medieval times

---

Buying Tips/Checkpoints

Genuine old oak:

- Old oak will have pit-saw, side-axe or adze marks. Adze cuts appear as scallop marks, while pit-sawn wood has triangular, irregular markings. Shine a shallow light on the timber to see these, which appear as gentle incisions: marks that are clearly overdone probably indicate fakery. For adze marks you are looking for marks about 2in (50mm) long by 1½in (38mm) wide all down the length of a beam. Adzes were generally used for smoothing timber after the main cuts had been made.
- The cross-sectional centre should be a chocolate colour.
- Wood should be very heavy – oak is twice as heavy as softwood, around 50lb per cu ft.
- Should be very hard – a hammered 6in nail cannot penetrate it.

Checkpoints:

- Ensure the timber is strong enough for its purpose – you may need a structural engineer's advice.
- Exposed (exterior) oak beams were traditionally painted black, or left unpainted; they are not polished wood.
- Check for wood rot, in particular deathwatch beetle (⅛in/3mm holes). As mentioned previously, woodworm is not an issue with oak: bygone 'dead' attacks (1/32in/1mm diameter holes) are often evident on the outer surface of old beams, and rarely affect the heartwood. 'Wet rot' is relatively easy to treat by drying out the timber and cutting out obvious decay. The more serious 'dry rot' (white strands and coloured fruiting bodies) is rarely found in oak. Deathwatch beetle is hard to eradicate and requires a specialist service, not just a standard pest exterminator, so avoid timber displaying evidence of this – typically ⅛in (3mm) diameter holes.

Close-up to show the tongue of a mortise-and-tenon joint with decay, but still perfectly strong – the rot only penetrates a short distance. (Courtesy Abbots Bridge Home & Garden Renovation Centre)

Close-up to show the end of a timber beam with surface rot only – if it's lasted a few hundred years already, it will go on for another hundred at least! (Courtesy Cox's Architectural Salvage Yard)

Apotropaic Marks

- Butterfly-shaped cross symbols – confusingly these were also used by carpenters for referencing plumb levels. Blacksmiths also used the butterfly cross on door latches and window-stays to repel evil.
- The initial M alone, sometimes with an adjacent R for Regina (Queen) or AMR (Ave Maria Regina) or MARIA.
- Multiple Ms frequently occur on chimney beams, often appearing in groups of three, which may have magical significance, as well as to symbolize the trinity.
- A single scribed W, like double Vs, signifying the Virgin of Virgins.
- Daisy wheels with six petals in a circle. Symbolic of the sun, but also had wider stellar implications in the sixteenth century.
- Circular marks containing a Maltese cross.
- Pair of scribed Os with a linking arc, like a pair of spectacles, their intention being to avert the evil eye.
- Three-sided symbols like a star within a circle (triquetra) otherwise triangle.
- During the sixteenth century the marks that refer to the Virgin Mary and other Catholic markings relate to medieval symbols pertaining to this, rather than directly to this religious symbolism.

onwards. Never use sandblasting, a blowlamp or a machine sander for this, as these are likely to irrevocably harm the surface; hand-sanding is likely to be not only time consuming but ultimately ineffective.

Remove tar from timber by using a chemical poultice, following the manufacturer's instructions. For removing whitewash, wash the surface with clean water and finish by brushing with a wire brush. Dirt can be removed from old beams by using a stiff brush, or you can try applying soap and water with a small amount of household washing soda, then washing the surface down with clean water. To remove paint from interior beams, or tar or paint from exterior ones, it's best to use a chemical stripper. Whitewash can be removed from beams by washing with clean water and rubbing down with a wire brush. Do not use wire-wool.

Defrassing

A very useful information leaflet from SPAB is *Timber Treatment – a warning about defrassing and surface treatment* (see Useful Contacts). Providing you're sure that any wood-boring insects are no longer active, a better alternative to defrassing is to leave the decayed material in place and apply six coats of a solution of PVA adhesive thinned with water on to the surface by brush, allowing each to dry. This adhesive penetrates the grain and effectively binds the damaged timber together and gives it a rock-hard surface. Otherwise, if you feel you really have to remove the frass, professionals remove this with an adze, and the yard selling the timber may offer this service. Alternatively you can use a hand-held axe, chopping sideways, but this has to be very sharp and must be continually sharpened. Again, do not use mechanical tools, as these will leave unattractive marks. Once the rotten sapwood (frass) is removed, (usually about ¼ to ½in/6–12mm only) you are left with the beautiful heartwood.

Treating Surfaces

External oak beams were not always meant to be painted or treated, but if you want to colour them, SPAB recommend that you use limewash: one method is to apply the limewash, and when it's dry, lightly brush it off, thereby leaving it in the crevices. However, limewash is unsuitable for treating interior beams or woodwork – for instance on ceilings.

Never paint old beams with gloss paint or bitumen-based paints, or use linseed oil. For interior beams that have no surface finish, you can either leave them in their natural state, or mix beeswax with turps substitute, then paint this on to the beam's surface, let it dry and buff it up with a cloth. Do not use any kind of varnish, including Danish oil, which contains a varnish-like component.

Huge metal uprights, obviously once used for structural support. (Courtesy MASCo Architectural Salvage Yard)

EXPERT ADVICE

Dale Sumner, of Ribble Reclamation

The older the oak, the harder it becomes – we call it bombproof! We do a 6in nail test for people who don't believe how hard it is. You cannot knock nails into it because it is like iron. Chainsaws manage one or two cuts before they have to be resharpened. We specialize in cleaning old oak and have managed to come up with one or two methods to finish the material to a very high standard, with a wonderful wax finish. Using a big beam over a fireplace is usually fine, but some building inspectors may not allow other structural applications, so a solution is to use a steel beam disguised by oak members.

Timothy Easton, artist/architectural historian

To see apotropaic marks you sometimes need to use a powerful torchbeam, shone crossways at the correct angle. They occur repeatedly around hearths, doors, windows, staircases and storage areas. Often there are two depths of cut, the deeper one, made by a carpenter's rase knife, frequently being the only one noticed by the householder. Lighter marks, made by a scratch awl or knife, can also represent part of a ritual carried out by the carpenter. Often the deeper and shallower carvings are combined together. Nearly all these marks were applied in the framing yard by the craftsmen, done generally when the timber was fresh.

Master carpenter and timber-frame construction expert, Wayne Kirby, of J. & W. Kirby

Don't confuse apotropaic marks with 'rush-light burns'. Typical sites for such burn marks might be at the dark area at the top of stairs. You can date a building by how many carpenters' marks were used, and the different styles that pertain to different periods.

David and Pat Reynolds

The Reynolds live in a sixteen-century timber-framed house in Yorkshire. David says:

We've often seen the marks on the beams and wondered about them. As well as carpenters' marks there are these strange 'compass'-type ones, which presumably are evil-averting marks I heard that they used to burn witches on the hill on which our house is built. In one part of the house a carpenter freaked out when the bubble on his spirit level wouldn't go between the centre lines, when it was obvious to both of us that he was holding it at true level!

Pat continues:

David's father used to say that when they had gas lights upstairs, someone unseen would blow them all out at night – there was never a draught that could have done it. Otherwise there's nothing sinister about the place, and maybe there never was. On the other hand, maybe the evil-averting marks are doing their job?

Peter Barker, of Antique Buildings Ltd

Modern saws leave modern (mostly unattractive) scars in the surface of the wood; bandsaws leave regular scars across the grain of the timber, whilst circular saws leave easily recognized curved scars. The random marks of an ancient adze or pit saw, softened by time, have a comfortable appearance which, in a home, may be enhanced by the gentle application of a little beeswax.

Elm has a wonderful grain with lots of character and swirl; historically it was used to make the seats of chairs as well as for flooring, but beware of any structure constructed using elm, as it is not a true hardwood – woodworm love to live in every part of it, and whilst it might look wonderful, its structural integrity just cannot be relied on. Oak, on the other hand, may often look raggy when the surface sapwood has been eaten away, but the chances are that under the first quarter inch or so the timber will be in perfect condition. Take care when buying beams that have been left uncovered in the rain for many years; the surface paints will have been spoilt by the weathering, and the heart of the timber will have become damp and susceptible to mould and insect attack, and is likely to have lost much of its strength. Having said this, plainly oak timbers survive perfectly well without being pampered. Most of the traditional farm buildings of England are built of oak; they are often open-fronted, and their oak timbers in perfect condition after hundreds of years.

In the house, the soft shine of beeswax is wonderful – it is soft to the touch and gives life to the timbers. If necessary, use one with a little stain to bring back colour – but always test first. Note that when first applied the solvent in the wax will give a darker effect before it dries. A gentle buff with either a shoe-polish brush or a cloth is usually all that is needed for perfection. Don't be tempted to use varnish on oak, as it really isn't suitable.

Nick Eveleigh, of EW Trading Ltd

If timber has been cut by a pit saw, on every plank there'll be a little triangular piece where it has been broken off. The marks are at about 30 degrees, a slightly angled cut mark. With old oak beams, sometimes you're lucky enough to have the chamfers on the main beams, and they can be dated by the stopped ends on those chamfers.

Douglas Kent, Society for the Protection of Ancient Buildings

In exceptional cases, what looks like dirt could be smoke blackening from the days of open fires that preceded chimneys, and it's a good idea for this to be retained. Avoid using steel wool, as unsightly rust stains can occur when metal fibres lodge in the timber's grain and corrode.

CHAPTER 4

Doors and Door Furniture

DOORS

Animal skins were the first means of covering entrances; subsequently the earliest 'battened' doors were made by joining a number of planks vertically along their edges, the joins in these early styles concealed by an additional batten on the surface. After Victorian times these joints could be overlapping, or tongue-and-grooved, with a V- (chamfered) section to mark the joint; alternatively they might have a beaded edge for this purpose.

'Ledged' doors were the simplest and earliest type of battened door, made from vertical boards ¾–1³⁄₁₆in (18–30mm) thick nailed to three horizontal rails known as ledges; another type was backed by an entire layer of horizontal boards. Prior to the 1700s when oak and elm were the timbers of choice, doors to the outside were normally of this robust construction, and were effectively two boards thick and nailed about every 4in (10cm) in a diamond pattern. Three nails were inserted in a triangular shape across the ledge on each board, because this formation effected the strongest bond: nails in a straight line would allow the planks to drop. The nails were also 'clenched', meaning that the projecting tip was hammered flat, so that they wouldn't move, affording additional support. Seemingly crude to us now, the practice was nevertheless extremely effective.

'Ledged-and-braced' doors were a nineteenth-century addition to ledged doors, whereby the ledges had diagonal timbers (braces) fixed between them, so as to provide additional support. Framed ledged-and-braced doors had a surrounding frame

at the sides and top, jointed together, creating an extraordinarily solid construction.

Panelled doors have thin timber panels that fill the spaces created by the structure's framework of horizontal and vertical timbers. 'Hanging' and 'closing' stiles are the uprights, linked by horizontal rails: the 'lock rail' is in the middle, while a 'frieze rail' divides the top two panels from the middle pair. Shorter 'muntins' link the rails vertically at the centre. The panels were made of thin hardwood or plywood slotted into surrounding loose-fitting grooves, and were never fixed. Mouldings were frequently used to cover the panel-to-frame joints; these were either proud of the surface, in which case they would normally be 'bolection' mouldings, or alternatively fitted flush. Otherwise the surrounding frame edges were contoured to hide the join. The bottom panels of entrance doors were often made thicker than the others for enhanced security, and were sometimes flush with the frame. Most Georgian doors have six rectangular panels, and occasionally have five or seven, whereas Victorian examples usually have four.

Glazed doors refer to those with panels of glass, which was often etched. This etching process involves using a stencil so that all but the cut-out area is protected from the sand-blasting process; alternatively the design is protected by the stencil and the background etched. Acid-etched/brilliant cut glass is a process whereby the entire surface is burnt with acid to produce a frosted effect, after which a design is etched into this, the resulting lines standing out in vivid contrast. A 'starburst'

LEFT: **Old ledged door.**
(Courtesy Abbots Bridge Home & Garden Renovation Centre)

RIGHT: **Old ledged door and frame. Note the rose motifs on the frame and the iron nail heads.** (Courtesy Architectural Salvage Source)

Glazed door with marvellous etched design in the glass.
(Courtesy Cox's Architectural Salvage Yard)

Glazed and panelled front door, with large raised mouldings covering the panel joints. Be aware that if you buy an old glazed door, it may not meet current safety standards. (Courtesy Abbots Bridge Home & Garden Renovation Centre)

Smart glazed front door.
(Courtesy Cox's Architectural Salvage Yard)

door is a particular type of Victorian design, where a stained-glass panel has green stars cut into its corners. Safety is an important issue, the reasoning being that glazing below a certain height could be hazardous to children. If you buy a second-hand glazed door it may not meet building regulation safety standards, so always consult a professional glazier if in doubt. In listed buildings some glazing may be exempt from the building regulations, but check with your local conservation officer to be certain.

Second-hand doors are approximately the same price as new ones, but old doors are likely to be more solid, and made of better timber.

Glossary

architrave Mouldings fixed to the frame that surrounds the door – two sides and a top length, mitred at their joints, whose purpose is to cover the joint between the timber doorframe and the wall.

bolection moulding Type of moulding around panels that stands proud of the background, with a distinctive profile that is partly rounded and partly straight.

casing The timber lining of an internal door opening, comprising two vertical jambs and a top horizontal soffit.

doorcase The structure, usually timber but sometimes masonry, that surrounds an exterior door on the outside wall. Elaborate examples may have vertical pilasters, brackets or even columns that support a door hood, almost forming a porch.

external doorframe The timbers surrounding an external door fixed to the surrounding masonry, comprising vertical posts fixed to a horizontal head (which may also act as a lintel, supporting brickwork above) and sometimes a bottom wooden threshold.

fanlight The glazed panel above a door, usually fan shaped and decorative, and set within the doorcase.

fielded panel This has a raised centre and is bevelled off at the edges.

flush bead Type of thin decorative moulding around panels, its top surface flush with the door's surface.

flush door With perfectly plain surfaces on both sides, this was an Art Deco invention, the earliest made by gluing solid wood strips together vertically, then fixing a plywood sheet to each side, with concealing hardwood lippings along side and top edges.

framed flush A flush door that is not solid throughout, reliant on an inner framework of timbers.

jambs Structures forming the vertical sides of an opening.

Ledged-and-braced door A ledged door with diagonal bracing timbers linking the three horizontals.

ledged door Made of vertical boards nailed to horizontal ones (ledges).

lintel Horizontally placed structural member which spans a door or window opening, supporting the masonry above.

moulding The profiled timber covering the joint between panels and timbers.

panelled door Comprises a framework of timbers with panels filling the holes so formed.

rebate Recess cut from timber, for instance to house the depth of a hinge.

'shooting' a door The practice of planing a door's edge to facilitate accurate fitting within the frame.

tongue-and-groove *See* previous chapter.

Practicalities

You will have to accept that it won't be easy to find a door that's an exact match to the remainder in your house, and it's equally unlikely that you'll find a matching set for wholesale replacement of all your doors. If you can't find a suitable second-hand door, consider having a door made to match.

In old houses doors are usually 'settled' so it is usual to have an odd shape to work with, meaning that the door will only be in proportion in certain parts. Unless you have a door made to measure, when the craftsmen can make adjustments to combat this kind of problem, a certain degree of disproportion may be something you simply have to accept.

ABOVE: **Part of Cox's selection of doors. Cox's possibly have the largest collection of second-hand doors in southern England.** (Courtesy Cox's Architectural Salvage Yard)

OPPOSITE: **The vast range of doors at Abbots Bridge yard.** (Courtesy Abbots Bridge Home & Garden Renovation Centre)

BELOW: **Part of MASCo's door collection, with a massive stone portico in sections on the ground.** (Courtesy MASCo Architectural Salvage Yard)

Replacing a Door

When removing the old door it's easiest to cut dried paint from the screw slots with a chisel, and use a suitably matching long-handled screwdriver. If the screw head snaps off or the slot is too shallow, drill a tiny hole in the screw head's centre, then use progressively larger HSS (high speed steel) drills to remove the remainder of the screw head, taking care not to drill down into the timber.

Trim or plane the door to fit, aiming to have a ⅛in (3mm) gap at top and sides and a ¼in (6mm) gap at the base. Always ensure your hinges are robust enough to support replacement doors, as old-style hinges are likely to be heavier than those used for modern doors. If the old hinges are serviceable (make sure they move freely and are not bowed or jamming), fit these to the new door's edge, first rebating the timber.

Finally screw the door in place: to begin with, use only one screw per hinge in the frame to check movement before inserting the rest. Use at least the same length screws as were used originally, or longer ones. If replacement hinges necessitate new holes in the timber, you may need to drill a small pilot hole in the frame before inserting the screw; if timber is especially hard this may need to be as long as the screw's length, but in most cases you're likely to need just a shallow-depth hole to facilitate the screw's initial entry. Brass screws are extremely soft, and always require the complete insertion, then removal, of a steel 'pilot' screw first.

You may need to plane the door for a final fit. 'Binding' as it closes is caused when the door's edge meets the frame on the hinge side at one or more points. If you can't see where the woods are touching, open the door and put a sheet of newspaper between the surfaces and close it: where the paper is trapped and cannot be easily pulled out indicates the problem areas. Mark these, remove the door and trim at these points.

If the door is rattling, the lock's keep is incorrectly positioned or loosely fixed, and adjustment or correction is the answer.

Stripping Paint

Lead paint may have been used in the past, so use a Nitromors lead tester kit (available in DIY outlets) before tackling paint removal, as stripping lead-based paint is potentially hazardous and is best left to a professional.

'Dipping' is a professional stripping service whereby the entire door is submerged in a bath of caustic soda; it is vital to ensure that the chemical is fully neutralized afterwards, otherwise corrosion

Timeline

14th/15th centuries	Front doors were generally batten doors, made of two planks, each approximately 14in (356mm) wide, joined at the back. The joint was covered with hardwood strips.
16th century	Hinges were positioned beneath the framing members on the door face, sandwiched between these and the door boards. Ornamentation was common on oak doors.
1690	Panelled doors first appeared. Early examples prior to 1710 usually had two panels and bolection mouldings. Doors were frequently square-headed with a four-centred arch, known as a 'Tudor' arch.
17th century	Cheaper softwood (pine) began to be imported from the Baltic, so elm and oak weren't used so much; as a consequence, doors made of this pine were lighter in appearance, though they still had heavy wooden frames and featured large locks. The boards for battened doors were now tongued-and-grooved together, or loose tongued or rebated, making cover strips unnecessary. Panelled doors were becoming more and more popular. H and HL hinges were used throughout this century and the next. Cock's head hinges were used. Internal doors were thin by comparison with later styles.
After 1750	Panelled doors with stiles and rails were becoming more common, and were now used in ordinary houses, not just grand ones. The most common type had two main panels, divided horizontally by a lock rail. Panels were fielded at edges, and had bolection moulding. Alternatively you could have two panels with a landscape in between, or eight to ten panels in large houses. Panels now might be arcaded and feature lozenges, diamonds and other such decoration.
Late 18th century	The number of panels increased to six, eight or ten.
1775	The cast-metal butt hinge was patented, becoming very popular by 1800.
18th century	In the Georgian period, the six-panelled door was the norm, the top two panels being smaller than those below. Butt hinges were developed. In the century's latter years, architraves were fluted and of rectangular section.
1810	Knobs or drop handles were in vogue for rim locks.
1850 onwards	Mortise locks were used and cheaper hinges were being made from stamped sheet metal. Victorian architraves were tapered mouldings, and mitred at the top.
19th century	Most Victorian doors were four-panelled, a style remaining popular ever since. Panels might be arched or circular, these types surrounded by wooden mouldings raised up on the surface. Glass panels were widely used, especially popular for entrance doors, where stained or acid etched glass was used for decoration. Glazing was generally confined to the upper half of the door, usually a single large panel, or occasionally there might be small panes divided by wooden glazing bars.
1850–1950	Fingerplates were in fashion.
1900	Bracing of battened doors began.
After 1918	Panelled doors became simpler in design, with mouldings no longer on the surface, and with panels recessed, these being made of solid timber or plywood.
1920s–1930s	Flush doors first appeared, a feature of the Art Deco movement. These were completely covered on both sides by plywood sheet or hardwood veneer.

Buying Tips/Checkpoints

Old doorframes are rarely truly rectangular, so measure your doorframe accurately, in three places horizontally and at the right and left side vertically, and always use the largest of these measurements. Reducing your new door's size is easy (unless you need to remove more than 1in/25mm), whereas enlargement is impossible. Also check floor levels and the squareness of your frame to ensure accurate matching.

- Check that the door is not twisted or warped.
- Make sure that joints are firm and the panels aren't cracked.
- Paint can conceal defective areas and broken joints, so examine surfaces carefully.
- With dipped doors (a drastic industrial process for removing paint by submerging the item in a bath of caustic soda) make sure there is no sugary deposit, indicating lack of neutralization of caustic soda; also make

Lovely glazed and panelled front door.
(Courtesy Cox's Architectural Salvage Yard)

sure that the joints are not defective, as the stripping process can dissolve old glue (see below).
- Glazed doors may not meet building regulations – you may need additional safety glass fitted.
- Ensure there's no rot or woodworm infestation; look especially carefully at the base areas. Woodworm is evidenced by a series of holes approximately $\frac{1}{32}$in (1mm) in diameter. Dry rot exhibits fungus-like white strands and/or coloured fruiting bodies; wet rot may show cuboid cracking or be evident as dark mushy or crumbling areas.
- For front doors make sure that the frame isn't weakened by large cut-outs for a mortise lock.

Very attractive front door made from reclaimed pine. (Courtesy Cox's Architectural Salvage Yard)

continues in perpetuity. Dipping can also sometimes destroy the old animal glue used for door assembly, necessitating the door's reassembly. DIY paint-stripping methods are labour intensive and messy, the options being to use a hot-air paint stripper or a chemical stripper. Again, before you start, always check for the presence of lead, as stated above.

Loose Hinges

A hinge's position may have been changed several times in the past, resulting in several large holes merging together, which prevents effective screw grip. The answer is to use thin dowelling timber and shape this into tapering pegs with a chisel. Then hammer the PVA-glued tapered dowelling pieces into the holes – they must be a very tight fit: you need to actually hammer them into position. When the adhesive has set, trim the dowelling flush to the timber's surface, then you can screw into the timber wherever necessary.

Disassembled or Loose Joints

Scrape away any debris and inject PVA into the gap, then close the joint using a sash cramp (this can be hired). Joints are sometimes loose when they are weakened or broken, or possibly because wedging pieces have gone missing. Grafting fresh timber into gaps may solve the problem.

Bowed Moulding

If a moulding is bowed, gaps will be left around the panel edges. Re-nail the mouldings in their correct positions, or replace them.

Warped Door

Identify the component of the door that is warped, and replace this. If the warping is not very noticeable you can try removing the doorframe's doorstop batten, identify where the door meets the frame, and trim the doorstop batten to meet this profile. Another idea is to reposition the hinges, altering one in relation to the other.

Split Panel

Splits occur more often on the panels of internal doors than external ones, and the crack is often

---

Trade Tips

- Save the dust from a door you've sanded – you can mix this with varnish or cellulose lacquer and use the resultant paste as a filler for tiny cracks.
- If you're going to wax the door, first seal it with one coat of polyurethane varnish: this provides a better base for the wax and binds the loose fibres together.
- Always seal bare timber to lock in its natural moisture, otherwise you may get subsequent cracks and splits.
- For a striking effect, polish the door and paint its frame.

---

along the butt joint of pieces that were glued together to form the piece. Sometimes a nail clipping a panel's edge or a build-up of paint can lock the panel in place, preventing natural movement. If this kind of restraint is removed, you can then screw planks to the panel face on either side of the split, squeeze in PVA adhesive, then clamp the blocks together to close the gap. If the panel cannot slide within its frame, enlarge the split enough to accept a graft of compatible timber, glue this in place, and afterwards trim this down flush with the background. Alternatively, tap a wedge-shaped piece of glued timber into the split, allow the adhesive to dry, and trim the wood back in the same way.

EXPERT ADVICE

David Crowley, of Aladdin's Antiques (reclaimed door specialists)

A door can be absolutely sound but have cracked panels, or the frame can be twisted but the panels are fine. So I transplant one to the other. Original old pine doors are normally stripped in a caustic bath, which reveals any defects, but the harsh alkali needs to be neutralized afterwards to prevent ongoing corrosive action – this could be apparent as a white 'sugaring' of the salts rising to the surface. Check that all joints are firm, and that the door isn't twisted. A tip for anyone waxing a door

Modern hardwood door with beautiful carved panelling, which looks just like a genuine antique. (Courtesy Cox's Architectural Salvage Yard)

Six-panel pine door with porcelain furniture. (Courtesy Cox's Architectural Salvage Yard)

Grand-looking outsize panelled door. (Courtesy Cox's Architectural Salvage Yard)

is to put on a coat of thinned-down gloss polyurethane varnish first: this acts as a sealer to ensure against future warping. Doors were originally made of identical size to the frame, permitting the carpenter to trim away a penny's thickness all round. Another tip is to do one door at a time completely to provide inspiration for any other doors you may have had stripped.

DOOR FURNITURE

Door furniture is the catch-all term for knobs, handles, hinges, letterboxes (also called letterplates) and knockers, plus associated flanges and fittings. Suitable and attractive furniture complements a door aesthetically: it is a practical necessity that you'll meet every day, besides being the vital finishing touch to give a genuine period feel. There are some excellent reproduction items, and the best of these are termed 'continuous production' because they are made in the same way as the originals; on the whole, however, genuine items are preferable, since they have an indefinable quality acquired by

time, they may have a patina that is impossible to replicate, or, in the case of brass, be made of a particularly beautiful type of metal that's no longer available. As mentioned in Chapter 1, prices for top-of-the-range reproduction pieces are on a par with that of fully restored originals. Inferior reproductions are much cheaper, but will ruin a fine door's appearance.

Knobs are usually sold in matching pairs on a spindle, either as a 'mortise set' when the lock is within the door's thickness, or a 'rim set' where a rim lock sits on the door's surface. The knob itself comprises the actual handle plus its rose, and rim sets have no rose below the knob on the lock side. They are made from timber (ebony, walnut, beech, mahogany or oak), brass, cast iron, bronze, glass or porcelain. Brass knobs are either hollow (spun) or cast solid, in which case they often had a patterned surface, such as swirls or 'beehive' circumference ridges. Brass lever handles are usually solid. Typical handle styles are pear-shaped, mushroom and oval. Georgian knobs tend to be smaller than Victorian ones.

LEFT: **Eclectic assortment of knobs and knockers at Abbots Bridge yard.** (Courtesy Abbots Bridge Home & Garden Renovation Centre)

BELOW: **All kinds of knobs and handles.** (Courtesy Heritage Reclamations)

Fingerplates were traditionally positioned above the handles on both sides, designed to protect soft lead paint finishes from fingermarks; push plates were only on one side. Escutcheons were plates acting as a mask around the keyhole on timber, normally made of metal, occasionally crafted from china; they were either round, rectangular or teardrop-shaped. Escutcheons were either left open, with a key-shaped slot, or their opening was covered by a sideways-swinging cover.

Letterplates and knockers are made of brass or iron, knockers sometimes being of bronze. The earliest were small compared to those of today, to match the smaller-sized envelopes. Varieties include the postal knocker, the doctor's knocker as well as the lion's head and horseshoe knockers.

RIGHT: **Letterboxes and doorknockers.** (Courtesy Heritage Reclamations)

BELOW: **Black iron doorknockers – very chunky and heavy.** (Courtesy Heritage Reclamations)

Glossary

butt hinge The first hinge designed to fit between the door and jamb invisibly.

cock's head hinge An H-shaped metal hinge, each end of which resembles a cock's head.

doctor's knocker Type of letterplate that is large and sweeping, in profile resembling an inverted S.

doorknocker The standard type was mounted centrally at head height on to the muntin.

doorpull Handle (usually circular) fitted at waist height to an external door to pull it closed; normally a large brass ring.

drop-ring latch Latch operated by turning an iron drop-ring.

escutcheon Decorative plate that surrounds the keyhole, sometimes having a sideways-hingeing flap.

fingerplate/doorplate/push-plate Protective decorative metal plate, usually fixed above the knob or handle.

follower Hole through the lock through which the spindle passes.

H and HL hinges So-called because of their shape; normally made of iron.

keep Receiver for the bolt, fixed to the architrave.

latch Short horizontal beam, pivoted at one end, that drops into a hook fixed to the doorframe. The beam was originally made from timber and lifted by string passed through a hole in the door; the beam was subsequently made in metal.

letterplate/letterbox Invented in 1840; early examples were made in plain brass, later ones being elaborately designed.

lift-off hinge Made in two parts so as to allow the door to be lifted off over the hinge's pin.

mortise lock Lock that is fitted within the door's thickness.

mortise set Refers to a pair of knobs on a spindle, designed for a lock that fits within the door itself.

Norfolk/Suffolk/thumb-latch Vertical handgrip with a thumb-plate latch opener above.

postal knocker Type of letterplate, with a 'hammer' or long knocker attached.

push plate Plate fixed to the 'push' side of a door, to protect its surface from fingermarks.

rim lock Metal lock fitted on to one surface of a door.

rim set Refers to a pair of knobs on a spindle designed for a lock that fits on the door's surface.

rising butt hinge Designed so as to cause the door to rise as it opens.

rose Metal flange beneath a knob. Can be either loose, spinning freely, or attached to the knob by circlips, so the knob can still be turned.

sneck Lever that lifts a latch. In modern parlance this has come to mean the mechanism on a rim lock that you can operate to hold the lock's tongue either in or out.

spindle The square shaft that penetrates the door and lock.

spun A type of hollow brass, shaped by centrifugal spinning; items are usually made in two parts which are bonded together, this junction often concealed by a decorative rim, typically around a knob at its centre.

stock lock A rim lock encased in timber.

strap hinge Flat-iron device fitted to the face of the door and the jamb.

thumb-latch A large, strong handle sometimes fixed to a back plate; the handle incorporates a thumb-operated sneck that lifts the beam off the hooked stop on the other side of the door.

Since mortise locks are concealed their appearance is irrelevant, and you may as well use a modern mortise lock that utilizes the latest security technology. Historic rim (surface-fitting) locks, made of timber, brass or black-painted iron, can look beautiful and enhance your home's period authenticity.

History

Locks

Door locks were used in Ancient Egypt and were in common use by the time of the Roman Empire. By the fifteenth century locksmiths in monasteries were making ornate silver lock plates, ordinary ones being fashioned from brightly painted iron. The original keys to early locks looked like a giant toothbrush with a crook in it – you reached through a hole in the door with the key, which was shaped to tip wooden pins, which in turn allowed the bolt to slide back.

Henry VIII carried his own wooden lock – the 'Beddington Lock' – around, to be screwed nightly on to one of his many bedroom doors. Timber locks were heavy and obtrusive, and in use well into the nineteenth century, and were fixed to the door by four screws or bolts; they were made from a large slab of oak, inside which was a mechanism of steel or iron that moved a wrought-iron bar into the keep. The 'castle'-type key was 4–6in (10–15cm) long. These security devices were made by local people, meaning each was effectively a 'one off' design. The earliest type of wooden lock was called the Banbury lock, and the generic name for wooden locks is 'woodstock locks'. Timber locks weren't made after the end of the nineteenth century; they were replaced by individually crafted iron, bronze and brass items. Machine-made pressed-steel locks have been made since the late 1800s.

The first 'warded' locks worked by the profiled end of a metal key (the flag) turning the bolt, with projecting 'wards' inside the mechanism preventing any but the correct key from rotating. Unfortunately 'skeleton' keys (conventional keys minus their central projections) could trip a warded lock bolt, presaging the invention of 'lever' locks. When you turn the key to such a lock you are lifting perhaps two levers to a pre-fixed height, so that the gating inside the lever, which is attached to the bolt stump, can move across. Basic single-lever locks have been in vogue since the late eighteenth century, but nowadays multi-lever locks are the norm, and are usually required by insurance companies.

From 1690–1810, brass or steel box-type rim locks were popular, and these featured round or oval knobs. In 1778 Robert Barron invented the double-acting lock, relying on the sophisticated action of two separate levers. And in 1784 Joseph Bramah created the 'cylinder' mechanism with its small key, the forerunner of present-day locks. In

Close-up of an old iron double-door fastener.
(Courtesy Abbots Bridge Home & Garden Renovation Centre)

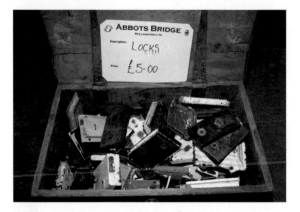

Old metal locks for sale – at this price you can afford to take a chance on it working properly. Keys can always be made by a good locksmith.
(Courtesy Abbots Bridge Home & Garden Renovation Centre)

1818 Jeremiah Chubb was granted the patent for a lock that detected small variations in the key shape: he even offered a reward to anyone who could pick a Chubb lock! By 1844 the Chubb lock was outdated by Linus Yale's new cylinder lock, a more secure device, operable by an even smaller key, which was cheaper to make and could also be mass-produced.

By mid-Victorian times the British lock industry was established in Willenhall, in the West Midlands. The varieties of door lock varied, from simple thin rim locks to large brass and gunmetal deadlocks. More sophisticated locks might have been enamelled or japanned (a lacquered finish).

Solid brass knobs with 'beehive' circumference ridges. (Courtesy Heritage Reclamations)

Fine collection of gleaming brass knobs.
(Courtesy Heritage Reclamations)

Doorknockers/ Doorknobs/ Letterplates
Doorknockers and knobs were widespread by the early eighteenth century, normally made of black-painted cast iron (brass was only for the finest homes). By Regency times the sphinx's head, lion's head and dolphin forms were common. Also door numbering was catching on – in London it had been obligatory since 1805. In Regency times much more door furniture was in use, and there was an increase in circular brass front-door bells. Interior doors had fingerplates made of brass, steel, glass or ceramics.

Letterboxes, also known as letterplates, came after 1840, to dovetail with the introduction of the penny post. The first were of cast brass, later examples being elaborately decorated. The first Victorian letterplates were tiny by today's standards, having a spring-loaded flap, often engraved with 'letters', and positioned either vertically or horizontally.

Hinges
The earliest hinges were hand-wrought by the village blacksmith. Styles included the 'strap' type, the assembly shaped like a T, whose long part was fixed to the door. By the late eighteenth century there were also H and HL hinges. H hinges consisted of two flat plates, one fixed to the architrave, the other to the door, joined by the hinge's spine. HL hinges had one long architrave side as a flat plate, while the other 'door' side was shaped like an L,

Hinges of all kinds, mostly of iron or steel.
(Courtesy Heritage Reclamations)

this angled projection helping to brace a heavy door.

Seventeenth-century hinges usually had decorative ends, later ones being plain. Butt hinges are let into the thickness of both door and architrave, a variation being 'rising butts', which raise the door to clear a thickness of carpet as it opens: these can be left- or right-handed. Georgian hinges were made of wrought iron, while Victorian examples were of thicker cast iron, after which pressed steel was the norm. Throughout the centuries brass hinges were traditionally used for higher quality doors.

History of Door Furniture Materials

Porcelain

Porcelain was first used on door furniture in the Victorian period. In 1851 John Pepper patented various mineral doorknobs, although they were only available in black, white and brown. They were made of porcelain mixed with a mineral to make it harder. Around 1890–1900, pierced porcelain fingerplates were made to match the porcelain knobs; the design of porcelain knobs changed, and a gold line was added to the plain white background.

Brass

Brass was first available in 1585 in the form of lattens – solid blocks of brass shaped into various household items such as bowls or basins. By 1595 brass was made as an alloy of copper and calamine, a red-coloured metal with a poor surface finish. Between 1690 and 1710, lead was added to the copper/calamine mixture, producing a softer metal that was easier to shape. In 1725 brass could be rolled by machine, then in 1770 James Emerson patented the alloy of copper and zinc that is similar to the form of today's brass. From 1860 onwards

---

Buying Tips/Checkpoints

- Carefully check ceramic parts for faults; crazing is permissible, as are cracks, providing the item's structural integrity is not compromised.
- If you want to fit a large knob, remember you'll need a deep-set lock, otherwise you will bark your knuckles. For locks that are close to the door's edge, a lever-type handle is more advisable than a knob.
- It can be very hard to find a large number of matching original mortise sets, so for some, good quality reproduction items may be your only option.
- Do not cut your door until you've got the letterplate, as hole positions are crucial.

Locks
- Ensure that spindle sizes and holes are all compatible and that they line up. These can vary a great deal, and holes for replacement locks are unlikely to precisely match those in your door.
- Spindle size is universal for British locks, but French spindles are of various different sizes that do not match British ones.

- Locks can be left- or right-handed, according to the way the door opens – make sure the replacement matches what you require.
- Don't worry if a second-hand lock has no key – a good locksmith can make a new key relatively inexpensively.
- Make sure you get the keep as well as the lock – very often the keep goes missing, as during demolition it is usually regarded as belonging to the door architrave rather than the door.
- The keep must match the lock – always check the keep's profile against the lock, as these are frequently mismatched when the correct one is missing.
- Ensure that the latch moves in and out and the spring is not broken. Steel locks can rust up inside, and when corroded they are prone to snap.
- Make sure the lock does not pre-date your property.
- For old timber locks, make sure that the steel mechanism inside hasn't broken. These can be repaired, but make sure the price you pay reflects this cost.

more complex castings were possible, therefore more ornate items could be made. Regency brass is often beaded, a typical item of Georgian brass door furniture being a plain knob on a round rose. The Victorians favoured swirls and highly decorative styles. There were basically two types of beading: a consistent small bead, and a pea bead – small beads alternating with longer ones.

Iron

Cast-iron door furniture was first known to be used in 1380, when it was brittle, plain and functional. Malleable wrought iron arrived later, offering more interesting designs such as leaf and spade shapes. Early iron door fittings were fixed with nails, and not screws. During the 1870s and 1880s, the Gothic revival period presaged a return of black antique ironware. This chunky door furniture is still used in churches and for large solid oak doors.

Signposts to Authenticity

- Old metals will show signs of wear and irregularity.
- Genuine old brass is a pinkish red, due to the greater copper content of old castings, while modern brass is a noticeably bright, brash yellow.
- Old knobs sometimes have a number stamped inside the rose, indicating an original patent.
- The internal iron of mild steel parts will be discoloured, perhaps rusty.
- Look for dirt or rust on grub screws.
- Examine metal for worn areas, denoting years of use.
- Cracked glazing on porcelain indicates authenticity, although this effect can be mimicked.
- Solid originals are usually heavier than new castings.
- Thicker iron, prominent fixings and elaborate decoration are typical Victorian features.
- Fingerplates should be of relatively chunky thick metal: crisply dressed thin metal denotes modernity.

Practicalities for Maintaining Metal Door Furniture

Stripping Paint

Check no lead is present by using the Nitromors lead tester kit, available from DIY outlets. If signs of lead are evident, stripping is best left to professional stripping companies. If no lead is present you can use chemical paint stripper, following the manufacturer's instructions – however you must wear suitable protective gloves and clothing.

Cleaning Brass

A dark patina is a sign of age, not of corrosion, and some people recommend leaving this. One traditional cleaning method is to sprinkle salt on to the cut surface of half a lemon and rub the metal with this to soften any corrosion. Alternatively you can use a commercial brass cleaner, but take care, because this is likely to contain surface-damaging abrasive materials.

Cleaning Rusty Iron

Soak the removed fittings in paraffin for some hours to soften the rust, then clean the surfaces with fine wire wool. Dry the metal and immediately treat it with a chemical rust inhibitor, prior to priming and painting; use a calcium plumbate or zinc phosphate primer followed by coat(s) of semi-matt black paint. Alternatively don't paint wrought iron, just wipe it occasionally with an oily rag.

Polishing

Use polishes sparingly, otherwise you will wear away the metal along with the dirt. For brass you can use a polish that leaves a chemical barrier on the metal that inhibits future corrosion.

EXPERT ADVICE

Clive Wilson, of
WRS Architectural Antiques

The Victorians were great innovators of ceramic knobs, for example using white with a surrounding gold band. They also liked black ceramic knobs and fingerplates, black iron and black ceramic items. They used many bronze and brass fittings that were subsequently painted. Many glass crystal knobs were inspired by the Great Exhibition of 1851. Fingerplates were usually rectangular and made from bone china, and they would often have scalloped tops and shoulders. Some were shaped at top and bottom, these designs being mirror images above and below.

The detailed methods of making door furniture using the 'lost wax process' are still a closely guarded secret in the Black Country. There are 'moulders' who made the mould and clay and wax templates. Then after the product is made, there are 'fettlers', who clean off the bits that stick out from the mould. Finally the component parts are polished and assembled.

Some of the Victorian hinges we find now are still as good as the day they were made. Dealers such as us have big boxes full of hinges – they really are stronger and better value than the modern ones.

David Kirk, of
Dorset Reclamation

Original doorknobs are always best, particularly if you can get a large number of originals that match. But remember, you don't have to match doorknobs throughout a house – having all different kinds of knob can add a lot of character to your home.

Linda Hall,
architectural historian

Earlier hinges tend to be plainer, less fussy than the later ones, which are more ornate with more nails. Reproduction items are often too thick and too fussy and have an unrealistic, shiny black pitted surface. Of course genuine arts-and-crafts pieces are also elaborate, but these are recognizably of that style and usually have finely detailed decoration and a smooth surface. Similarly, old seventeenth-century wooden lock cases were subtly fixed, perhaps with a nail at each corner, whereas more recent ones have got far more ironwork on them. Really old locks don't have any strapping on them at all, except very occasionally a metal escutcheon around the keyhole. Most had simple decoration such as a moulding top and bottom, or

carved notches down the ends. Eighteenth- and nineteenth-century ones may have fine incised lines around the lock case.

Anthony Reeve, of LASSCO

We always have an ever-changing supply of Victorian and Edwardian brass door furniture. It's superior to what is made today in terms of quality of engineering and materials. Old brass had a higher copper content, evident as a much warmer, richer colour than that of modern brass. Generally, solid brass is Victorian. If you're replacing door handles in a property, be aware that if the spindle goes through the door quite close to the frame, be wary, because in that arrangement you'd be better off with lever handles than knobs.

Apply oil or grease to the working parts of an old lock – this will prevent further rusting and corrosion. If it's easy to dismantle, do so and take off the surface rust, but don't be too enthusiastic: simply take off surface corrosion and nothing more. Then oil the parts and apply WD40, which offers good protection.

Charles Brooking,
architectural historian

Charles Brooking specializes in the study of building features and is the founder of the Brooking Collection (www.thebrooking.com).

Most Victorian rim locks were generally plain; elaborate types are likely to be American. The best quality rim locks were made of brass, and the majority of iron was 'japanned'. Upper-class houses had mortise locks for all the doors. In the late Georgian period mortise locks were used in grander rooms, and rim locks fitted for less important ones, for instance bedrooms; in more humble houses, however, rim locks were used throughout. 'Stock' locks were wooden-cased locks that were used right up to the 1930s, for garages, wine cellars and so on.

Mark Kitchen-Smith, of LASSCO

The nice thing about old brass is that, according to when it was cast, it had varying mixes and percentages of the constituent metals, copper and zinc, which distinctly affected its colour. Older brass is redder, a nicer, warmer, more mellow colour, whereas modern brass castings almost verge on a glaring greeny yellow. Old brass has the mellowness that complements old doors and properties. You notice if you find a piece of old brass that hasn't been cleaned for a while that it gets a very nice blacky-brown patination, which is a lovely thing to find. If you're restoring an old house you don't want fittings to glare out that you've just put them in.

Wooden locks aren't that expensive, but they do tend to break – springs are apt to get broken and go missing, and these can be repaired but it's sometimes not worth the expense. Old mortise locks are more trouble than they're worth, and since they're never seen you're better off buying new ones.

Master locksmith, Anthony Jarvis

The more ornate locks would have a higher value – for instance the old lavatories at stations used to have ornate locks on them, beautiful brass examples, with a slot for pennies. Warded locks were the first mass-produced ones, the more secure lever type originating in France around 1767, catching on here a little later. You should keep old locks in a nice dry environment if possible. Put oil or grease on the working parts, as this will prevent further corrosion. If the mechanism in an old wooden lock breaks it's a matter of getting a new one made from spring steel. For a key, the 'bow' is the part between your fingers, then there's the 'shank', then the 'collar' which prevents the key being inserted too far into the lock. The 'post' is the bit beyond the collar, prior to the flag where the 'bitting' goes.

SPECIAL DOORS

You can sometimes find quite rare and outlandish doors in salvage yards. These might come from churches, public buildings, grand ballrooms or even prisons, and can be of virtually any size. Clearly they're not suitable for the average property, but if you live in a castle or a stately home, they might easily be exactly what you need.

LEFT: These grand double doors were probably from a stately home – not quite right for a suburban semi.
(Courtesy MASCo Architectural Salvage Yard)

OPPOSITE: Prison doors – not something tailor-made for your drawing room!
(Courtesy Cox's Architectural Salvage Yard)

ABOVE: **At around twelve feet high (3½m) you'd be pushed to find a use for these magnificent timber-and-iron doors.** (Courtesy LASSCO Ltd)

TOP RIGHT: **Planning to film a gothic horror in your back garden? These giant doors should fit the bill.** (Courtesy LASSCO Ltd)

BOTTOM RIGHT: **These metal doors are larger than life – ideal if you have a castle or a vast gothic mansion.** (Courtesy LASSCO Ltd)

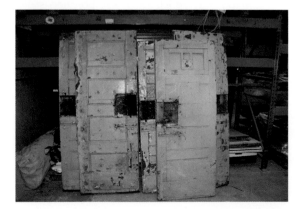

CHAPTER 5

Glass, Windows and Lighting

GLASS AND GLAZING

Glass lasts thousands of years, but sadly, when a building is demolished this all-too-easily breakable material is one of the first casualties. But if you can find windows containing their original glass, this is generally a far more attractive material than modern mass-produced glazing. Old glass is usually thinner than its modern equivalent, and contains minor imperfections which give vivid reflections as a result of the light being scattered and twisted in different angles and directions. This is a random beauty that cannot be replicated by modern glass: cloudy, snowy or sunny weather outside can set a totally different scene within a room, and the view from inside can be slightly distorted, evoking days gone by. Similarly, looking from outside, images seen through old glass can be extremely beautiful. It is ironic that two thousand years of improving technology, enabling the production of absolutely flawless glazing, means that the attractive idiosyncrasies of old windows have been lost.

The other components of windows – metal and/or timber – are prone to corrosion, meaning that many ancient and serviceable windows have been thrown away needlessly when they could have been repaired, and their glass has been scrapped as a result.

Glass has always been made by heating sand, silica, soda and lime together until it is a treacly liquid, then manipulating this into shape until it cools and solidifies. The early types of glass had many impurities and imperfections, such as surface irregularities (ream), curvature and small air bubbles (seeds) embedded in it. Until around 1832 it was not technically possible to make a large sheet of glass, meaning that prior to this, windows always required glazing bars; in fact in the early days of glass production only extremely small panes could be made (quarries), and these were joined via a framework of metal piping to make leaded-light windows.

Types of Glass

Broad Sheet Glass (aka Muff Glass)
This was the earliest form of glass, and was made as follows:

- The glassmaker dipped a long pipe into the pot of molten glass and drew out a gather of glass, which he then blew into a bubble.
- This bubble, still attached to the end of the blowpipe, was rolled on a flat polished stone (the marver).
- The bubble was then elongated by swinging it to and fro; then after various processes, the neck of this cylinder was spread until it was of constant diameter,
- It was then sheared open, flattened, and the sheets so formed allowed to cool in an annealing kiln.

Where you might find it: Old leaded lights, seventeenth-century (or earlier) iron-framed windows.

Glossary

bullion The central, swirling 'bull's eye' shape apparent on some crown glass caused by the attachment of the punty pipe during production. Originally considered to be waste material, but now prized.

calm or came Flat or half-round strip of lead of an H-shaped cross-section, a number of which are soldered together in a framework and used to surround the quarries for making leaded-light windows. The traditional spelling is calm(es), derived from the Latin calamus, meaning 'a reed'.

cartoon Full-size blueprint for an artist-designed window.

cement The putty or mastic filler between glass and lead cames.

crizzling The scaling of the surface of glass that impairs its clarity, often associated with fire damage.

flash A thick coat of coloured glass applied (flashed) to the surface of white or potmetal glass during manufacture. Flashing can be abraded or removed by acid to give two colours.

glazing bar Horizontal or vertical, round, square or T-shaped support for panels of glass within timber or metal frames.

grisaille Geometric leaf patterns of regular design leaded into, or painted on, white glass.

heart of came The inner lip of old cames on which the maker's name and a date might be imprinted.

leaded lights Large panels made up of relatively small panes of glass held in place by a framework of cames.

potmetal glass Glass coloured throughout its thickness, made by adding one or more metallic oxides as it is melted in the pot.

quarries Diamond- or rectangular-shaped small pieces of glass, the glazing components of a leaded-light window.

reams Attractive ripples apparent in the surface of very old glass.

seeds Bubbles caused during manufacture, that may be apparent in old glass.

stained glass Where the material is originally all one colour, other contrasting colours are hand-painted on to its surface, then the pane is fired in a kiln.

yellow/silver stain Stain ranging from orange to pale lemon produced by applying a solution of a silver compound, which, when fired in the kiln, changes the glass to various shades of yellow.

Crown Glass

Crown glass was first made in Normandy, then in England. The process was as follows:

- A gatherer dipped the end of the blowpipe into the molten glass through the furnace's mouth, and rotated it around until he had gathered a weight of glass.
- This was allowed to cool, then the process was repeated several times, progressively adding more glass to the original gathering until 8–9lb (3.6–4kg) (weight) of the material was attached to the pipe.
- It was rolled to and fro on a smooth iron plate (the marver) to make it cylindrical.
- An assistant then blew into the pipe to make the cylinder pear-shaped.

- The glass was reheated in the furnace, whilst simultaneously being rotated.
- The iron pipe (punt) was then attached to the molten mass, which was held in the furnace and rotated until it formed a flat circular panel called a 'table'.
- This was laid in a depression in sand and the punty broken away, leaving a characteristic 'bullion' mark in the centre.

This type of glass may therefore have a bullion mark, a brilliant surface, slight impurities and an irregular surface texture, and give reflective and refractive qualities.

Where you might find it: Georgian sash windows.

Timeline

3000BC	Glassmaking probably originated in Syria at around this time.
45BC	The Romans were presumed to have made glass in Britain – traces of Roman furnaces have been found, and small pieces of window glass have been excavated from most Roman settlement sites.
AD675	Bede refers to Benedict Bishop's appeal to Gaul (France) for glassmakers for glazing church windows.
1226	Broadsheet glass first made in Sussex.
13–14th century	A glassmaking centre was established in Chiddingford, on the Surrey/Sussex border. The glass was made from a potash flux produced from the ashes of bracken and beech.
1567	Elizabeth I granted a licence to Jean Carre, an Antwerp merchant, to manufacture window glass in Britain, and he brought over *gentilhommes verriers* (gentlemen glassmakers) from Lorraine to teach English craftsmen the trade of making broad glass.
1615	James I forbade by royal decree the wood-firing of glass furnaces, meaning that the coal-fired Reverbatory furnace had to be used instead; the key figure in glass production, Sir Robert Mansell, established Tyneside as his chief glass production centre.
1620	Plate glass was first produced in London, by grinding and polishing broad sheet.
1678	Crown glass was first produced in England. It was named after the small crown embossed on such panels made at the Bear Garden, Bankside.
1696	Crown glass was made more generally.
1746	Excise duties were put on glassmaking. The duty depended on the size and thickness of panes, but generally its effect was to make thinner sheets more economically attractive.
1750	Most window glass was crown glass.
1773	The first English factory to make polished plate glass was established at Ravenhead in St Helens.
1830s	Staircase windows often had coloured glazing.
1834	The improved cylinder method was introduced by the Chance Brothers, and cylinder glass became popular. Much larger sheets could be made in a process similar to that of making broad glass, the difference being that the cylinder was allowed to cool, was split with a diamond, then reheated and flattened.
1838	'Patent plate glass' was created by making polished cylinder glass thin enough to avoid being in a higher taxation bracket; this was also less distorted.
1845	Glass taxes were removed.
1847	Rolled plate glass was invented by James Hartley; it was made by ladling molten glass on to a table and rolling it.
1850–1900	Cylinder glass replaced crown glass generally.
1850s	It became fashionable to use glass in doors and door surrounds, frequently with the top two door panels being glazed with acid-etched glass. Natural or geometric designs were common themes, birds and flowers being popular. Bay windows of the 1930s to 1950s often featured a star or central sun design.

Cylinder Glass (Cylinder-blown Sheet Glass)

This was made by blowing a long cylinder of glass, cutting it along its length and opening it out flat. Its production was a somewhat similar process to that of making broad glass, the difference being that the manufacture entailed more processes, and enabled larger sheets to be produced. This could be made in larger sizes than crown glass, and soon after its discovery the window tax was repealed.

Where you might find it: In windows made from 1850 to 1900.

1870–1900	Larger sizes of cylinder glass could now be made, leading to different patterns of glazing bars in windows. Decorative glass in doors was commonplace, including coloured glass in patterning, and stained glass.
1889	A disc-grinding and polishing process for finishing glass was patented. These processes were performed on circular steel tables, 30–40ft (9–12m) in diameter.
1890s	Coloured glass in windows was used decoratively, and many terraces had front doors with decorative glazed upper panels: this was a typical Arts and Crafts feature, and continued until the 1920s and 1930s.
1910	The drawn cylinder process was invented by American John H. Lubbers, an automated procedure requiring little manpower and utilizing compressed air and mechanical methods of production.
1910	Drawn flat sheet glass was invented, also an automated process.
1931	Pilkington produced flat drawn sheet glass under a licence from the Pittsburgh Plate Glass Company.
1959	The float glass process was invented, whereby molten glass from the furnace floats along on a bath of molten tin and is kept there at a high temperature for a time, so as to allow the glass to assume the perfectly flat surface of the tin, and for irregularities in the glass to melt out. The resultant surface is flat and parallel.

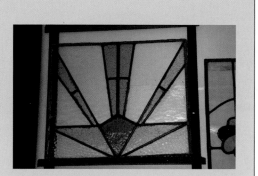

Leaded light panel. (Courtesy Cox's Architectural Salvage Yard)

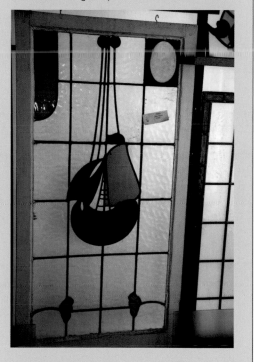

1930s Art Deco glass. (Courtesy Cox's Architectural Salvage Yard)

Plate Glass

'Blown plate' was first produced by polishing thick cylinder glass for making the finest glazing – for mirrors, stately homes or coach windows. Then 'polished plate' was developed. The glass was poured onto a table and then ground and polished, first by hand, then by machine. This eventually superseded blown plate glass.

Where you might find it: Quite rare; it is found in old mirrors and windows glazed before 1650.

LEFT: Decorative stained glass panel in a wooden frame. (Courtesy Cox's Architectural Salvage Yard)

BELOW LEFT: Victorian hand-painted stained glass panel. (Courtesy Cox's Architectural Salvage Yard)

BELOW: Another Victorian hand-painted stained glass panel. (Courtesy Cox's Architectural Salvage Yard)

Modern Glass

Drawn sheet glass was invented first, then finally float glass, which is poured on to a bed of molten tin, producing a flawless, perfect surface, but lacking individuality.

Stained Glass

Correctly this is termed 'stained and painted' glass, and describes the process whereby a painted design, using oxides or enamels, is fused into the surface of the glass (frequently already coloured) by kiln drying. 'Staining' pertains to characteristic silver stains producing tones from pale lemon to deep amber, applied to the reverse face and fired in. There is a stained glass museum based in Ely Cathedral, with all kinds of work on display (see Useful Contacts).

The process has hardly changed since the

twelfth century. Initially painted details were in black or brown paint, then in 1300 yellow was discovered, which enabled white glass to be turned yellow, or blue glass green – useful in the highlighting of hair, haloes and crowns. The practice continued into the eighteenth century, then the craft declined and the skills were lost until the gothic revival movement (Arts and Crafts), when stained glass was rediscovered and proliferated.

The colours in a stained glass window usually come from the numerous separate pieces of coloured 'potmetal' glass selected and cut for the design. Fine details such as facial features, drapery folds and hands are hand-painted in brown, black or grey vitreous 'glass' paints on to the surfaces of the individual pieces, which are then kiln-fired to fuse the paint to the potmetal surface permanently. In addition, tones of yellow can be 'stained' on to the glass by a special firing technique involving silver chloride.

Genuine antique stained glass has a beautiful depth of colour and quality of finish. Second-hand panels can be used to reglaze a window (oversize examples can be cut down) or hung in front of an existing one. Alternatively you can make a 'stained glass windowsill' on which to display antiques, or a matching pair of stained glass windows can be hung on a wall, mounted in a frame.

Leaded Lights

Small pieces of diamond- or rectangular-shaped glass (quarries) are held together by a latticework of lead strips (calmes). Originally used in early (fifteenth-century) glazing, when only small pieces of glass could be made, it was then reintroduced during the Arts and Crafts period, key Victorian proponents being Pugin, William Morris, Burne Jones and Mary Lowndes, not to mention many other Victorian artists and designers. Often these quarries would be artworks of stained glass.

Acid-etched Glass

Acid etching is where flash-fired mouth-blown glass has a colour fused on to it. Acid was then brushed over specific surface areas to selectively remove layers of colour, like a painting in reverse. Sand-blasting gave textured effects.

Antique Glass/Mouth-blown Glass

This type of glass is handmade and contains bubbles, ripples and irregularities. It is generally thinner than modern glass.

Opalescent Glass

This type of glass is produced by adding chalk to the glass mix. It gives good reflections for Tiffany lampshades.

Cathedral Glass

This term often refers to modern machine-rolled glasses, coloured all the way through. The process was first used in the early 1840s to describe a lightly tinted sheet glass with a slightly textured surface.

Buying Tips/Checkpoints

- Buy from a reputable dealer.
- Inspect the panel carefully, as originality is vital.
- Small cracks, even broken pieces, are better than bad repairs.
- Similarly don't worry about bumps, lumps, ridges, colour variations, misshapen pieces or air bubbles – these are signs of antiquity.
- In leaded lights look for cracked leadwork, buckling and bowing.

Practicalities

- Leaded lights can be cleaned by using a paintbrush, whilst simultaneously extracting debris with a vacuum cleaner. If harsher cleaning is needed, try an alcohol-based cleanser – one such is 'glass cleaner' made by Hodgsons Sealants.
- Clean quarries individually, within their cames, rather than sweeping over the entire panel.
- Never paint lead caming, as its naturally acquired grey-black acquires its own attractive patina.
- Gaps around quarries can be filled with leaded light cement, also from Hodgsons Sealants.

Building Regulations

New glazing has to meet Part L of the Building Regulations, requiring a minimum level of insulation. However, you do not have to meet this rating if you are replacing windows like-for-like in a listed building unless you are adding an extension, in which case the new glass has to conform to Part L.

Doors, door side panels and glazing below 31½in (800mm) from the floor level are designated as 'critical locations' and glass fitted here should meet government safety requirements. Modern toughened or laminated glass that meets BS6206 has to be used in these positions.

- Grease can be removed from antique glass with an old shoe brush, newspaper or a lint-free cloth.
- Generally for cleaning old glass avoid standard window-cleaning solutions. Clean organic growth, such as lichens, algae or fungi, carefully using a neutral PH soap. Avoid potentially harmful biocides. Do not use detergents, bleaches, caustic soda, ammonia or acids, and protect the glass if you are using any of these on the surrounding window frame.
- If the glass is painted, don't clean the painted side, because if the paint is not stable you might remove it.

EXPERT QUOTES

Drew Pritchard

Sometimes the value of a restored window can far outweigh its restoration costs. If a piece of stained glass has a crack or two, it doesn't matter – it's better to leave these alone than to risk further damage by dismantling the whole thing. Originality is like gold dust. If something's incomplete or comprised of non-matching replacements you'll always have problems. It's better to have an unadulterated piece, even if it does need some renovation, than an incomplete or badly restored one.

WINDOWS

The name evolved from the old 'wind eyes' or 'lights' set high up just under the eaves and covered with parchment or waxed paper. In the late sixteenth century valuable leaded-light glass served this purpose. Reclaimed windows are either sold 'as seen' or restored by the dealer, and generally speaking are cheaper than new ones. The problem is likely to be with dimensions, as these were never standard, although some dealers may

Steel window frames. You can strip and treat the metal yourself and a glazier can easily re-glaze them for you. (Courtesy Cox's Architectural Salvage Yard)

Range of steel window frames, some glazed. (Courtesy Cox's Architectural Salvage Yard)

ABOVE: **Large wooden window frames.**
(Courtesy Cox's Architectural Salvage Yard)

RIGHT: **Random collection of wooden-framed leaded light windows, probably dating from the 1930s.** (Courtesy Mongers Architectural Salvage)

BOTTOM RIGHT: **Complete steel-framed leaded light window with lovely coloured glass.**
(Courtesy Cox's Architectural Salvage Yard)

cut down larger cast-iron windows to size. Making your hole larger is impractical, as this will reduce the necessary side support for the lintel above, however it may be possible to infill each side of a smaller window, if you can match the masonry. Alternatively, if you are extending an older house, you could get the windows first and tailor your design accordingly.

Timber casement windows comprise the majority of what is available second-hand, however some yards have Georgian cast-iron ones, and 1930s-style 'Crittall' windows are also available. There are plenty of UPVC windows (complete with double-glazed glass) available, and these can be excellent buys. Some dealers may have stone (mullioned) windows, largely from demolished churches, but these are rare finds. On the whole, timber windows can quite easily be restored, and a good blacksmith can restore damaged ironwork.

When considering very old windows, one distinct advantage is if they still retain the original, beautiful glass (*see* earlier section on glass, p. 76).

Unfortunately second-hand sash windows are a rarity; however, if you find them, but working parts are missing, there are companies that make all these items; there are also several specialists who renovate sash windows and can make them draughtproof.

Windows framed in cast iron are much more solid than those with steel frames, and their glazed areas tend to be comprised of small glass panes, held together in a latticework frame; glazing bars are bevelled or round-faced on the inside.

Standard shapes of stone windows are rectangular with an arched or pointed top, or square, or sometimes even round. Sandstone is the most usual material, but limestone and granite are occasionally used. Tall stone windows might be divided vertically into lozenges called 'lances'. The interior faces of the stone sections are rebated to accept the metal frame that surrounds the glass, and this cut-out is called a 'redlet'. A stone window is comprised of the base sill, one or more vertical 'jamb' sections, plus top pieces, fixed together with mortar, occasionally also pinned. The sections from which it is made sometimes have keyways in the end of the stone to accommodate cube- or rod-shaped pieces of slate, and joined using lime render as an adhesive.

Many owners of period houses and some surveyors and architects intensely dislike UPVC windows, disparagingly referred to as 'plastic' windows. Apart from obvious aesthetic issues, where, sadly, they've been fitted inappropriately to an old property, it is said that making these products adversely affects the environment; but if you are buying second-hand items, they've already been made, so this argument does not apply. Despite these criticisms, a vast number of properties throughout Britain, typically dating from the 1930s,

Range of brass-and-steel window furniture.
(Courtesy Heritage Reclamations)

Attractively designed leaded light window in a wooden frame. (Courtesy MASCo Architectural Salvage Yard)

Glossary

cam fastener Closing device made up of a rotating metal arm tongue on one window that engages in a fixed plate receptor on the other.

casement stay Flat metal bar pivoting against the lower rail of the frame, for propping it open in various positions.

cockspur fastener Where a handle on the window is attached to a tongue that engages within a plate fixed to the frame.

espangolette bolts Rod-type bolts with a central handle, for French windows.

extension hinge Projecting hinge that creates a 4in (100mm) gap between the window and jamb when open, allowing access to the window's exterior for cleaning from the inside.

ferramenta The ironwork that forms the surrounding structure for old timber- and stone framed windows, examples being hinges, window stays and opening handles.

fitch/crescent fastener Similar to the cam fastener, but with a semi-circular tongue of increasing thickness that aligns the rails precisely as it locks them together.

light Ancient term for window, sometimes used to mean one of the two component panels of a sash window.

saddle bars Horizontal support bars in medieval windows, to which window leadwork was attached by a lead wire.

sash One of the two key panels of a sash window (see below).

sash handles Handles fixed to upper frames.

sash lift Metal plates, recessed (flush lift) or surface-mounted (hook lift) for raising the lower sash.

sash screw Threaded screw with a turnable flat handle that passes through both rails, for securing them together in the closed position.

sash stops Can be fitted to one of both sides to restrict the sash's opening.

screw fastener A knurled nut screwed over a pivoting threaded pin that pulls and locks the frames in place.

spalling (blown) Name given to the cracking of stone, caused by embedded ironwork rusting and expanding.

sprig Tiny flat nail used to retain glass within timber frames.

---

have had replacement UPVC windows fitted, and these look fine, and are weatherproof and thief-proof. Many UPVC windows are also available second-hand.

Good plastic windows, whether second-hand or new, are long-lasting, will not rot, and, due to integral metal structures where support is needed, are perfectly adequate structurally. Second-hand UPVC windows can look as good as brand new plastic windows, and cost a fraction of the price. They may also have a timber frame and/or sill attached, meaning more money saved, if you want these extra items. They will also benefit from the additional insulation advantages of double glazing, but check with your LA as to whether they will comply with Part L of the building regulations.

Modern UPVC and new timber windows cost about twice the price of their second-hand equivalents, whereas new Crittall windows are similarly priced to renovated second-hand ones.

Types of Window

Bay: A window with sizeable side panels so as to form a projection outwards from a room, thereby adding extra space and increasing the light.

Bow: Window that projects outwards in a shallow curve.

Casement: Side-opening windows (usually one or sometimes both sides), with iron or timber frames.

Crittall window: Casement-style steel windows first made by the 1930s firm Crittalls, now being manufactured in the original way. Simply flat glass panels mounted into panes surrounded by framing with a T cross-section to accommodate glazing on either side.

Dormer: Window(s) in a roof.

Double-hung sash: A window where two 'lights' move independently and in unison, joined by a system of pulleys and weights.

Fixed light: A medieval construction, whereby leaded lights are either framed by wrought-iron rectangles or fixed directly to the outside. It is non-opening.

Mullioned: The earliest, pre-glass type of window, with vertical stone or timber mullions (bars) separating the opening; the sides of these uprights were often angled so as to admit more light. Horizontal transom bars were sometimes added. A stone-mullioned casement is side opening.

Oriel: A box-like window projecting from an upper floor and supported on brackets.

Sash: Two wooden (or originally metal) frames surrounding glass (lights or panels); the frames slide against each other vertically. The single-sliding sash is where the upper light is fixed and only the lower can slide, whereas the more usual double-sliding sash is where both frames move in tandem with each other, counterbalanced by a system of ropes on pulleys and weights.

UPVC: Modern 'plastic' windows.

Frame Materials

Metal Frames

Medieval to 1794	Wrought iron
1800–1886	Cast iron and wrought iron
1886–1955	Ungalvanized steel, prone to serious corrosion
1955–present day	Galvanized steel

Wooden Frames

Pre-1720	Oak
1720 onwards	Softwoods – although ancient 'softwood' was considerably stronger than such timber today.

Sash Windows

The double-hung sash has a box frame that surrounds the two movable sash panels. Hollow on both sides, this frame is divided vertically to form two chambers, which house the moving parts. The counterweights, balanced so their weight is equal to that of their respective sashes, are joined to them by ropes or chains that pass over pulleys; the counterbalancing effect ensures smooth movement. They are locked closed where they meet at

---

Timeline

Medieval	Mullioned windows used on larger houses, with no glass.
Late 16th century	Leaded-light glass was used in non-opening iron-framed windows, and later in side-opening wooden casements, which arrived at this time. Oriel windows were also used, and bay windows were installed in grand houses.
1669 (approximately)	Thomas Kinward, whilst being employed by Sir Christopher Wren, developed the box-framed sash window, which is still being made today.
Mid to late 17th century	Sash windows came into use more generally – notably in Inigo Jones's Banqueting Hall (1685).
1702	The casement window was by this time more or less superseded by the sash.
1750s	Bow windows arrived.
18th century	Twelve to sixteen panes per window panel was usual, divided by glazing bars.
1850	Double-hung sashes became popular. Bay windows were ubiquitous in urban terraces.
Late 19th century	Four or two panes per window panel became the norm, thanks to improved glassmaking techniques.

the centre by means of a catch. The panels were made up of panes divided by glazing bars originally, but by the beginning of the twentieth century the panels were a single pane.

Practicalities

Removing/Replacing Old Glass
from a Window Frame
Using a chisel invariably leads to breakages. Instead use an infra-red lamp (these can be hired from Roger Mears Architects, see contact details at the end of the book) to soften the material, allowing you to carefully remove it, without scratching the timber or damaging the glass by heating it too much. Direct the lamp at the putty at a 45 degree angle, and protect the glass with a damp cloth. For wooden frames, remove the glass-retaining glazing sprigs (tiny flat nails) to release the glass, then shave away putty from the wood's rebate using a sharp chisel. Prime bare timber before reglazing, and use linseed-oil putty for the bedding and face material.

Mix the putty thoroughly by kneading it between your fingers: it is ready to use when you can insert and remove a finger without feeling anything sticking to your skin. First work the putty around the window's rebate with a thumb (the bedding), press the glass into that, then carefully nail in the sprigs, leaving a tiny gap so as not to put uneven pressure on the glass, which would crack. Apply the front putty, smoothing this to a flat angle

Large sash window. (Courtesy Abbots Bridge Home & Garden Renovation Centre)

Problems and Solutions	
Seized or broken pulley	Replace the pulley, or remove any paint clogging it and/or lubricate the wheel.
Broken cords	Replace all cords at the same time, never just the broken one.
Stuck shut with paint	Run a knife along the area and apply a poultice-type paint stripper.
Beads out of line	Refit them.
Swollen or warped timber	Plane to size. Make sure there are no unpainted areas that can absorb water and cause the timber to swell.
Rattling	Have the units draught-stripped by a specialist.
Loose joints	Remove glass, disassemble frames then rebuild, re-gluing the joints. Some old animal glue can be softened with kettle steam.

with a dry putty knife (ensure that the line does not come higher than the internal rebate). Use a clean dry brush on the putty's surface. Finally flow primer paint slightly proud of the putty line to give a waterproof seal.

For metal frames, the glass was often set into a steel-framed window by putting a bead of putty in first (bedding), then the glass, followed by a metal stop that was quadrant shaped in cross-section. Alternatively there might be a Z-shaped metal spring clip that holds the glass in place, which will be covered by putty. When replacing glass it is vital

to have more than simply putty alone to support the weight.

Renovating Timber-Framed Windows

Casement window frames are made up of two vertical stiles and top and bottom rails, connected by mortice-and-tenon joints, which may incorporate wedges. A hinge is fixed to one side. Glass panels may be divided by wooden glazing bars, or may be made up of a panel of leaded lights. Settlement can cause problems such as jamming or breakage. This may be caused by a decayed lintel above the window – consult a surveyor for advice if you suspect this may be the case.

Wet Rot, Dry Rot, Woodworm

For large areas, remove the minimum amount of timber, and after treating the remainder, fix pieces of matching wood (ideally reclaimed timber of around the same age) by gluing and fastening it in position with non-ferrous screws or pins. Smaller areas can be treated by removing the affected area, treating timber with suitable preservative and woodworm or rot-deterrent preparation, then filling with a proprietary exterior wood filler, such as the two-pack resin-based kind. Sometimes a combination of both approaches can work well.

Loose Joints

Remove the glass, then dismantle the joint, clean and sand the exposed areas, then re-glue, packing with more wedges if required, and clamp until dry. For additional support you may like to add a non-ferrous angle bracket.

Loose Hinge

This is likely to cause sticking and jamming. Remove the window, then drill new (countersunk) holes in the hinge plate and re-screw into position.

Sticking

Plane off the excess material, avoiding taking away too much timber. Swelling is likely to have been caused by the wood's absorption of moisture, so it is vital to prime and paint the timber so as to seal its surface against further absorption.

Renovating Metal-Framed Windows

If there is serious corrosion of the hinges or handle it is best to remove the unit, take out the glass (see above) and have the frame professionally restored. Steel-framed windows are either screwed to the surrounding timber frames, or metal lugs that are bolted to the frame are built into mortar joints.

Other problems can be distortion, excessive paint build-up, failed hinges and fittings, and corrosion. Defective putty can suck in and retain water, as can a compromised seal around the perimeter. Correcting a bent frame or hinge can possibly be done by brute force. Small corrosion holes can be filled with a resin-type two-pack metal repair compound.

Stripping Paint and Rust

Always test any old paint you are about to remove with Nitromors lead tester in case lead is present; if it is, take suitable precautions. Wrought iron can be heated with a welding torch flame, allowing you to wire-brush debris away. Don't heat cast iron, as this may crack (for how to delineate between these two, see the section on ironwork, p. 142). Alternatively, remove debris by wire-brushing cold, then use an acid-based rust remover.

For steel, a sharp wood chisel should slice away the material: as soon as the metal is bare, protect the surface with primer, as rust forms almost immediately. You can remove light rust with silicon carbide paper dampened with white spirit; collect the dust with a cloth soaked in methylated spirit. For heavier rust, wire-brush until you reach solid metal, and fill any pitted areas with metal filler.

UPVC Windows

When you are picking from a stack of these windows, the frame is likely to look dirty and possibly off-white. Once you've washed them with soap and water and scraped off any adhering cement or plaster (with a blunt chisel), clean the frames with specially made UPVC solvent cleaner, applied with a kitchen scourer pad. Before the liquid dries, wipe it off with kitchen paper or a clean cloth, and repeat as necessary. This usually brings back the whiteness of the frame almost as good as new. The

windows are screwed either to a timber frame set into your masonry, or directly to it. Fill any gaps with good quality exterior frame sealant – cheap frame sealants are unlikely to retain their colour over time, and may not adhere well.

EXPERT QUOTES

Drew Pritchard
(on reclaimed stone windows)

Stone is the most expensive material to repair by far, plus it's extremely difficult to find people with the expertise to do it. When you look at a stone window you have cusps, where the points of the stone come together. It's very common for these to be broken, so check these especially.

Eve Guinan, of Minchinhampton
Architectural Antiques and
stained glass expert

Surface rust on metal windows is fine, but if the metal is corroded, jagged and worn, don't buy it. Make sure a metal frame is square and not buckled. If there are metal glazing bars, make sure these are complete. Don't worry if ordinary glass is missing or incomplete – reglazing this is relatively simple and inexpensive. For timber windows, check for rot, especially at the base.

Ben Sinclair, of Norgrove Studios

Judge the integrity of leaded lights by crooking your finger and carefully tapping the pane with your fingertip. If loose, rattling and mobile, this indicates the panel needs rebuilding. If we were to do a complete rebuild the window would have to carefully come out and it would then be cartooned, dismantled, cleaned and re-leaded off site, but for replacing odd panes it's possible for a specialist to peel back the lead, extract the old damaged glass and insert a replacement glass to match the existing surviving glass. Remember – introducing modern float glass to existing leaded lights will be disfiguring. It is also generally thicker, and therefore difficult to fit within the existing lead alongside thinner handmade glass. If the panel appears stable with a number of broken panes, then consideration should be given as to whether removal and serious repair would give a better result than *in situ* patching, as the physical integrity of lead will be compromised.

Roger Mears, of
Roger Mears Architects

Old wooden windows were made by hand, so repairing them, rather than replacing them, means you're saving that wonderful hand craftsmanship. Old timber, whether hardwood or softwood, has vastly superior qualities to modern timber as it is denser, with more heartwood and less sapwood. This older, slow-growth heartwood is of hugely greater durability than any modern timber.

LIGHTING

Many reproduction light fittings are of very high quality and are extremely realistic, but do not have the enhanced value of a genuine antique. Nor can they have the touches that only years of use can bestow: a patina to the metal and a level of craftsmanship that would not be cost-effective today. The only way to be certain that you are getting an antique is by buying from a reputable dealer; otherwise there are various pointers to authenticity.

Candles and rush lights were the earlier forms of lighting until the 1850s, when paraffin was discovered. In the Middle Ages candles were usually made of tallow, produced from mutton fat, and were smoky and malodorous. The portable socket candlestick was introduced in the sixteenth century; prior to this, candles were held in wall sconces or 'candle beams' – large crosspieces of wood fitted with metal bars. In richer houses, mirrors might be put behind wall candle sconces to increase the illuminative effect. In the eighteenth century impressive crystal chandeliers first appeared, but they required so much maintenance, and so many candles were needed, that even in grand houses these beautiful lighting devices were only lit for special occasions.

Oil lights gradually replaced candles, then gaslights replaced oil lamps. Innovations didn't instantly destroy their predecessors, but coexisted for years, the newcomer only gradually ousting the one before. Electricity was considered damaging to health and likely to cause insomnia, and gaslights were considered vulgar even though they were 'free from the inconvenience of sparks and the frequency of snuffing'. Candles were still used for domestic lighting until the early 1900s – notably as a portable form of lighting for bed-

Chandelier in need of care and attention.
(Courtesy Mongers Architectural Salvage)

Nadine Davis repairing an antique crystal chandelier. (Courtesy Architectural Forum)

rooms. Country houses would have 'lamp rooms' for the storage of assorted lighting paraphernalia, where 'lamp and candle men' would polish and scrape wax off candelabra, clean the glass chimneys of oil lamps, and cut wicks. Torchères served the same function as modern-day standard lamps, the early ones made of iron or wood. Lights that hung from the ceiling – otherwise known as 'pendant' – were originally called chandeliers. Chandeliers might be as rudimentary as candleholders on an iron circle supported from the ceiling by chains, or as magnificent as a splendidly ornate, brass Flemish-style chandelier with elaborately curving arms, perhaps festooned with pieces of cut glass.

The earliest Victorian electric fittings were based on gas and oil lamp designs, with an unshaded bulb mimicking an oil lamp's glass chimney. Bulbs might be of any size or shape, even engraved. The original 'Edison' bulbs were somewhat dazzling until the concept of lampshades became accepted. The original Victorian fussy creations were replaced by the graceful, simplistic designs of lamps and fittings during the Arts and Crafts era. Art Nouveau fittings and lamps frequently featured leaves and flowers or slim beautiful women. Classical Revival styles, after Art Nouveau, emulated the Georgian ideas of Adam, Hepplewhite and Chippendale. Straightforward pendant light fittings might have had silk or glass shades, or fabric skirts. Upside-down cut glass or alabaster bowls, set in decorative brass or bronze mounts and suspended on chains, first appeared with gas lighting and were ubiquitous in Edwardian times; however, more bulky variations on these ideas were everywhere in the 1930s. Electric pendant lights normally had the arms directing light downwards, as did the wall lights, in contrast to the gas lamp and candle chandeliers, whose arms curved upwards. Shades for Victorian table lamps were made of glass, or of pleated and gathered silk.

ABOVE: **1930s-style pendant lights with white dome shades.** (Courtesy Cox's Architectural Salvage Yard)

BELOW: **Chandelier with cut-glass drops. If drops are missing you can usually get replacements from specialist suppliers.** (Courtesy Architectural Forum)

Beautiful glazed lantern. (Courtesy Cox's Architectural Salvage Yard)

Glossary

chandelier Any multiple light that hangs from the ceiling, including chain-supported candleholders on an iron circle, ornate Flemish-style brass ones, as well as those festooned with droplets of cut glass.

chimney Cylindrical glass with a bulbous section, open at each end, used inside the globe or silk shade on oil lamps and some gas fittings.

cranberry glass Very beautiful, subtly coloured pinky-red glass made in the Victorian era, by a process of infusing 24-carat gold into molten glass.

craquele glass Thick glass with a crackled outside finish, often used to make ball globes for figure lamps of the Art Deco period.

doctor's lamp Desk lamp, usually made in brass, with a horizontal trough-shaped swivel shade in metal or green glass.

femme-fleur Style of Art Nouveau table lamp, depicting a woman in flowing clothing entwined with leaves and flowers.

flambeau Lampshade made of opaque or tinted glass moulded into the shape of a flame.

gallery Circular metal plate or dish with a lip with three or more screws, that fits above or directly on to the lamp holder and holds a glass shade in position via the screws.

gasolier Chandelier made for gas lighting.

girandole Ornamental wall candle sconce, normally incorporating a mirror.

lantern Originally a box to protect a candle flame from the wind; also used for gas and oil lamps. In the 1920s and 1930s lanterns made from cheap metal were used as hall and landing lights.

lustres/drops The shaped pieces of glass dangling from a crystal chandelier.

milk or enamel glass White translucent glass often used for lampshades. Appears similar to white porcelain.

opaline A semi-opaque translucent glass that gives rosy hues when held to the light. Made in pastel colours, frequently displaying special effects of iridescence and translucence.

pendant Any light that hangs from the ceiling.

rise-and-fall Type of pendant light fitting counterbalanced with weights and pulleys so it can be raised and lowered as required.

ruby glass A clear, deep ruby-red glass made using gold chloride.

Nadine Davis adding the finishing touches to a Flemish-style brass chandelier.
(Courtesy Architectural Forum)

sconce Wall-mounted wall sconces were originally made as a way of maximizing the light from candle-holding arms projecting from a reflective metallic backing plate, which might be polished bronze, copper, ormolu or gilded gesso, shaped as a shield or oval, sometimes with attractive pictorial designs. This reflector could also be a mirror.

Tiffany lampshades Extravagant and attractive shades, made up of a patchwork of brightly coloured glass panels. Originated in the Art Nouveau era, created by the artist Louis Tiffany.

torchère Floor-standing lamp, similar to a modern-day standard lamp. Early ones were made of iron or wood, with a bowl to carry the lamp or torch, or holding up to twenty candles.

Vaseline glass Yellowish-green material that appears amber when illuminated. Now in increasingly short supply, because it cannot be made today – it was originally made by infusing uranium into the molten glass. Its colour can vary from opalescent cream to a brilliant translucent yellow.

wall sconce Developed from the chandelier wall sconces, where arms projected from a reflective metallic backing plate, made of bronze, copper or ormolu, or alternatively a mirror.

Chandelier with cut-glass drops.
(Courtesy Architectural Forum)

An excellent book on lighting, which was largely the source for the glossary and some of the other information here, is Josie Marsden's *Lamps and Lighting*, by Guinness Publishing Ltd: it contains all the information about the subject you could ever possibly need. Although it is out of print, you may well be able to track down a second-hand copy, or your library might have one in stock.

The usual rules concerning price apply to historic lighting fittings: bad reproductions will be relatively cheap, but the price of good ones will equate to that of properly restored originals.

Buying Tips/Checkpoints

- Examine the item very closely; never judge from a distance.
- Indications of a reproduction are modern screws, different proportions, longitudinal joint lines, obvious soldering and casting marks.
- Electrical safety is absolutely paramount: always budget for complete rewiring costs, and have a fitting checked by a qualified electrician before using it; only total dismantling tells you if a fitting is safe to use.
- Avoid an item that has perished brass, as this cannot be repaired.
- Genuine old brass is deep yellow, whereas modern brass, indicating a reproduction, is more orangey.
- An original's finish might be silver, bronze or gold.
- Avoid an item that has been highly polished – this means that the original finish has been removed, and its value will be diminished.
- Reproductions tend to be lighter, because cheap examples are made of pressed, rather than cast, metal (originals were made from cast metal).
- An antique light is unlikely to be suitable for a bathroom, as special safety rules apply, principally that all electrical parts have to be fully enclosed. However, fittings that were designed to be fully enclosed might be suitable, as can fully enclosed old Art Deco lights. Always check with an electrician if in any doubt.

EXPERT QUOTES

Hector Finch, of Hector Finch Lighting

Look out for badly restored fittings. People might spend a fortune on something, not realizing it's some cobble-up assembled from parts from three different items – what I call a 'mix-and-match fitting'! Search for modern screws, places where things don't look quite right. Look for obvious soldering, different metal colours, screw holes in funny places, odd proportions. Never judge something hanging from the ceiling from eight feet away – get close to it. Remember, the unit may work perfectly well, but inside the wiring can be deadly dangerous. Rewiring is expensive, and a reputable electrician will refuse to fit anything unsafe. Avoid something that's been polished. Originally these items were made of brass, which always had some kind of finish: this might be a dark oxidized colour, bronze, silver plate or even gold lacquered. An old gold finish will produce a subtle colour, reminiscent of an antique scientific instrument. Never polish such finishes away, for that destroys the value.

Josie Marsden, of Magic Lanterns at By George

Judging whether something is antique is a matter of the feel of it, its quality and its general look. There's an awful lot on the market that is falsely classed as antique. Someone might mistakenly describe an item as Georgian, or Tudor, when what they should really say is that it is of that era's style. Anything electric is likely to be post-1900, so electrical fittings prior to that are normally converted from a gas fitting. A fitting always has to be completely dismantled before you can know if it's electrically safe.

Christopher Wray, of Christopher Wray Lighting

When people say 'I want to light my house' they rarely differentiate between the beauty of the fittings themselves – for instance, lovely old antique lamps or modern aesthetically pleasing fittings – and the actual light they deliver. These two qualities should always be considered separately. So in a period house you can put in beautiful brass antique lamps, but also use subtle modern lighting to provide more light, or even to illuminate the antique lamps themselves. Plus you can always use antique lamps in a modern house, or vice versa, or any mixture of the two.

Get the wiring in an old lamp checked by a qualified electrician. It's normally best to get it rewired anyway, for safety's sake. When rewiring, ask your electrician to use silk-wrapped flex, which has more of a period feel than standard flex and comes in a variety of colours. Good quality old lights are increasingly hard to find, but they are still available, while original glass shades, whether for old oil lamps, pendants or wall lights, are very much scarcer. Generally speaking it's impossible to find a match for a pendant which has three arms but only two shades. In such circumstances it's better to sell the originals and buy three matching reproduction ones. Missing chandelier drops are fairly easy to replace, but if you have an unusual style, replace them around the light and fill in the gaps equally with other similarly styled drops.

Ray Kelly, of Kelly Antique Lighting

Look at the configuration and the fineness of the castings. For instance, try and unscrew a bottom acorn or something as a way of seeing inside. You can then see if its interior is of shiny new brass, suggesting recent manufacture. Reproduction brass is rather orangey, not the deep yellow of the genuine article, imparted by the old metal's zinc content. The chief difference is that the old lamp fittings were made when labour cost almost nothing. To reproduce something in the original way would cost around £5,000 for labour in today's market, so it's not surprising that original antiques are so prized. Genuine Vaseline glass is extraordinarily beautiful – as wonderful to look at unlit as when it is illuminated. Take a close look at the whole thing, and if you think 'How could they have made that?' then it's likely to be an old one. With genuine antiques you do not see any joint lines – they were all filed out and buffed away. Cast reproduction examples are made by continuous casting, and you can see the casting marks as occasional longitudinal joints in the body.

CHAPTER 6

Fireplaces, Chimneypieces, Radiators, Flagstones and Floor Tiles

FIREPLACES AND CHIMNEYPIECES

The first type of open fire in houses consisted of a pile of burning logs on the centre of the floor of the open hall, the smoke dispersing through a hole in the roof above. Later on, the fire was made against an outside wall, and a canopy of stone or plaster-and-lath built above to gather the smoke and allow it outside, through a hole in the wall. This latter arrangement was the forerunner of the inglenook (meaning chimney corner) fireplace, a sizeable chamber approximately 6–8ft (2–2½m) wide, above which was a large chimney that led to the roof. Seats were sometimes added in the alcove on each side of the central burning area; iron firedogs supported the logs, allowing air to circulate beneath. The fire served for cooking as well as heating, and bread ovens were sometimes incorporated.

By the eighteenth century the inglenook had become smaller and cooking facilities were not required – these were transferred to a separate fire in the kitchen. Cast-iron baskets or dog grates contained the wood, and the whole thing was enclosed by surrounds, which might be of carved wood, marble or stone. Mantelshelves first appeared at this time.

Chimneypieces, fireplaces and grates from the past are available fully restored, in their unrestored state, or produced as reproductions, and the usual pricing rules apply.

Grates

All grates were basically a basket device to contain the combustible material (originally wood, latterly

An old iron bread oven, fully restored.
(Courtesy Cox's Architectural Salvage Yard)

Beautiful old hob grate, with hob plates for pans and kettles. (Courtesy Heritage Reclamations)

Glossary

canopy Hood that may be attached to a recessed fireplace, its purpose to gather the smoke for the chimney.

chimney Structure surrounding one or more separate flues.

composition A mixture of materials such as whiting and glue, used to fashion raised decoration on a chimneypiece, picture frame or similar timber item.

corbel Angular decorative support that forms a feature in itself, typically at each side, under the mantelshelf.

fireback Lining to the builder's opening behind the fire, serving the dual functions of protecting the masonry and reflecting heat back into the room.

flue The void of passageways through which the combustion products are removed from the fire to the outside.

footblocks Blocks at the base of a marble fireplace on which the jambs stand.

frieze Horizontal panel below the mantelpiece, that links the jambs.

grate Fireproof box in which combustible material is placed.

hearth The fireproof raft on which a grate or fireplace stands.

'in the paint' Trade term meaning the item still has its original paint finish.

jamb(s) Vertical side pieces of a mantelpiece.

mantelshelf/mantelpiece Shelf forming the horizontal top of the chimneypiece or fireplace. Mantelpiece can also mean the entire chimneypiece as a unit.

sugaring/going sugary A defect of marble, whereby the material can split apart with no warning.

LEFT: **'Before' shot of an old iron fireplace with surface rust removed, just before being sprayed with anti-rust paint.** (Courtesy Abbots Bridge Home & Garden Renovation Centre)

BELOW: **Stove paint being sprayed on to the fireplace shown in the previous photograph.** (Courtesy Abbots Bridge Home & Garden Renovation Centre)

RIGHT: **Rare 'radiolette' cast-iron stove, with the name 'Godin' in decorative lettering.** (Courtesy Heritage Reclamations)

BELOW: **An old iron fireplace prior to being renovated.** (Courtesy Abbots Bridge Home & Garden Renovation Centre)

coal) and raise it above the hearth, so as to allow air's circulation; it thus served the same function as firedogs.

Dog grate: The first was the dog grate, basically a metal basket on legs, with iron or steel bars in front; it was developed for coal use as opposed to wood.

Hob grate: Next was the hob grate, smaller than its predecessor, with a smaller raised grate and hob, or shelf, at each side, to provide a facility for heating pots and pans – hob plates. It took up the bottom half of the opening. Early hob grates had brick sides to the grate area and a sloping brick channel or flue leading up into the chimney. They had wide decorative front panels and a high fire basket.

Register grate: The register grate was an advance on the hob grate, its chief feature being that it had a front plate or panel that filled the entire opening. Early ones had cast-iron side panels and back. There was a closer plate above that sealed off the chimney opening, and a

section of this was covered by an adjustable register plate, allowing you to adjust the amount of heat loss up the chimney. Polished steel register grates dating from 1790 might have a wide basket with small side hobs with a decorative apron beneath.

The insert grate: This has the same arrangement of covering the plate with a front panel, but no register plate.

The arched grate: This featured an arch instead of a squared top, and had a smaller fire basket set at a lower level, no hobs, and a splayed, coved interior.

The splay-sided fireplace had a narrow rectangular opening with splayed sides decorated with tiled panels; the fire basket was set very low and front bars lifted out as a unit, and an ash pan fitted beneath.

Finally the tiled register grate arrived, which was a register grate with panels of tiles incorporated down the sides and a hood or canopy over the fire, which was often adjustable.

LEFT: **A very old chimneypiece, from Rotherham Ironworks factory – you can tell it is cast iron from the bare metal at the base of the jambs.** (Courtesy Abbots Bridge Home & Garden Renovation Centre)

MIDDLE LEFT: **A restored iron fireplace.** (Courtesy Abbots Bridge Home & Garden Renovation Centre)

BOTTOM LEFT: **A wonderful old fully renovated fireplace, complete with fire irons.** (Courtesy Abbots Bridge Home & Garden Renovation Centre)

BELOW: **Beautiful iron chimneypiece with tiled cheeks.** (Courtesy Cox's Architectural Salvage Yard)

Cast-iron Chimneypieces

These were fireplaces and mantelpieces combined in one unit. The unit was either made of concrete faced with marble or plain tiles, or from brick. The grate was a separate bolt-on fitting.

The cast-iron parts were normally black; grate polish was used to give a surface shine. Some had a finish like shining steel, referred to as 'burnished': brass and copper parts were often incorporated in these burnished types. Famous maker names include Coalbrookdale and Carron. Do not buy an incomplete cast-iron unit – it is usually impossible to find the missing parts, and there were hundreds of different makers. Exceptionally, missing firebars can sometimes be matched by reproduction items, or spare firebars are sometimes stocked by salvage dealers.

ABOVE: **Cast-iron insert with marvellous old tiles inscribed with the days of the week and accompanying designs.** (Courtesy Cox's Architectural Salvage Yard)

TOP RIGHT: **Cast-iron fireplace with floral tiled panels.** (Courtesy Cox's Architectural Salvage Yard)

MIDDLE RIGHT: **Cast-iron chimneypiece with tiled cheeks.** (Courtesy Heritage Reclamations)

BOTTOM RIGHT: **Pretty cast-iron fireplace with pink floral tile panels.** (Courtesy MASCo Architectural Salvage Yard)

BELOW: **Showing the magnificent detailed design on a complete cast-iron chimneypiece.** (Courtesy Architectural Forum)

ABOVE: **Elaborate and majestic marbled chimneypiece, with a cast-iron grate.**
(Courtesy MASCo Architectural Salvage Yard)

BOTTOM: **Marble chimneypiece with cast-iron insert and tiled panels.**
(Courtesy Heritage Reclamations)

BELOW: **Detail of marble chimneypiece, showing the intricacy of the carving.**
(Courtesy MASCo Architectural Salvage Yard)

ABOVE: **Wonderful white marble chimneypiece with green marble inserts.** (Courtesy MASCo Architectural Salvage Yard)

TOP: **Large marble fire surround – the cracks have been successfully repaired and add charm and authenticity to the piece.**
(Courtesy Abbots Bridge Home & Garden Renovation Centre)

BELOW: **Fine black marble chimneypiece with cast iron fireplace.** (Courtesy Mongers Architectural Salvage)

Marble Chimneypieces

Marble chimneypieces are usually made up of four sections, assembled on site: jambs at the sides, and mantelpiece and frieze horizontally above, with the jambs sitting on footblocks. Regency examples often have a 'bull's eye' – basically two roundels below the mantelpiece at each side – whereas Victorian types would often have corbels in these positions. Italian white marble (Carrara) has light grey veins running through it, and is the most highly prized. Grey marbles are usually French or Italian. Examine the mantelpiece carefully, as any faults here will be prominent. Marble is a natural material and accordingly a few defects are to be expected.

A damp atmosphere can cause marble to become compromised, a condition colloquially referred to as 'going sugary', because the material feels like granulated sugar to the touch. Affected material can split apart and fragment for no reason: this fault can be detected by an expert who taps it, a hollow sound indicating the worst. As a rule, a marble chimneypiece is set 1¼in (30mm) into the wall's surface.

Stone and Slate Chimneypieces

Grand stone fireplace – probably from a stately home or castle. (Courtesy Heritage Reclamations)

The earliest stone fireplaces were an intrinsic part of the building's structure, whereas in Georgian times they were mounted separately on the chimneybreast, and the mantelshelf often did not project. Limestone and Bath stone were typical choices, but granite was not used. Slate fireplaces were often given a painted imitation marble finish complete with veining, usually black or green.

Wooden Chimneypieces

ABOVE: **Wooden chimneypiece with intricate carving. Separate cast-iron section of insert inside.** (Courtesy MASCo Architectural Salvage Yard)

BELOW: **Wonderful wooden chimneypiece with gesso decoration, cast-iron insert with tiled panels.** (Courtesy MASCo Architectural Salvage Yard)

Fifteenth- and sixteenth-century wooden surrounds were of oak and usually have later additions. Georgian and Regency ones were mostly pine, rarely oak, and have a higher narrower mantel than marble examples; frequently these had decorative additions glued on – made from 'composition' that was moulded, or else carved from pear wood or lime wood. These additions might have been gilded or highlighted to make them stand out. Wooden fire surrounds would often have a white or coloured wash applied over the timber, which allowed you to see the grain. These constructions were made up of panels glued together for fitting as a complete unit.

Practicalities

Fixing Chimneypieces to the Wall
A marble chimneypiece is fixed to the wall using steel wire ties, or hooks bonded into the back

---

Timeline

Grates

Medieval	Logs placed in the centre of room, smoke released through a hole in the ceiling.
15th century	The inglenook was invented.
1700s	The inglenook was reduced in size. Decorative fire surrounds and mantlepieces arrived, and the dog grate was invented.
1750	More decorative types of dog grate were being produced.
1760	The hob grate was invented, becoming popular by the end of this century.
1820s	Register grates were first used.
1840s–1880s	Arched grates were in vogue.
1870	Splay-sided grates became popular.
1880s	The tiled register grate, incorporating panels of tiles along its sides, became a familiar feature.

Chimneypieces

Late 1500s	Large houses had elaborate stone-built fireplaces and surrounds.
1700	More straightforward stone and wood surrounds were popular; mantelshelves were rare.
1750	Decorative columns (pilasters) were used as jambs. Elaborate rococo decoration was a common feature. Mirror glass in large sheets was now available from France, and used to make richly decorated 'overmantels'.
1830s	The influx of a variety of styles, including marbled surrounds. White-coloured marble and black slate were popular. Frequently timber was painted to simulate marble.
1800–1850	The use of tiles for decorating grates and mantelpiece became increasingly fashionable. A typical tiled Victorian fireplace had splayed-sided panels with five 6in (150mm) square picture tiles fitted one above the other, sometimes separated by patterned or plain half- or quarter-tiles. Some sets of decorative tiles, when assembled, made up a complete panel.
1860	Combination fireplaces were invented. These were elaborate and of cast iron, and combined grate, surround and tiled cheeks all in one unit. A burnished metal was becoming well liked as an alternative to black. Ornate overmantels with mirrored panels and fancy display shelves were fashionable.
Early 20th century	An Arts-and-Crafts influence dominated interiors, with oak, stone and brick making a return. The wooden panels were ornamented with Art Nouveau fretted brackets and panels.
1930s	Mainly marble, plain tile or brick was used; fancy tiled cast-iron grates were a thing of the past.

edge of the component parts; these fixings are set into the wall's plaster, or tied with wire to screws or nail hooks set in the wall. Cast-iron units have cast lugs at the top and bottom of the jambs for fixing to the wall with screws. Wooden ones are fixed with screws or nails fitted through metal plates attached to the jambs, similar to mirror fixings. Finally, plaster is applied to conceal the fixings and to help give support.

Buying Tips/Checkpoints

Marble
- Check for cracks and splits.
- Carefully examine the surface's veining and colour for unmatching areas, which might indicate a section has been replaced.
- Feel the surface for a 'granulated sugar' feel, which can indicate the terminal 'going sugary' condition.
- Search for stains. Rust stains are likely to be impossible to remove, whereas other types might be 'drawn out' using a poultice-type stripper.
- If you buy a chimneypiece that's already fixed to a wall, bear in mind that when it is removed it may fall to pieces – don't pay until it has been removed.

Stone and Slate
- Check for hairline cracks. Splits in some types of stone, particularly the darker ones, can be hard to repair.
- For slate, the painted surface is often discoloured and faded, giving the impression that there's trapped water beneath the surface. This surface patina cannot be cleaned, as it dissolves easily if disturbed.

Wood
- The more original decorative work the better.
- If the surface is painted and you strip this, you may easily find the timber's surface is charred, due to previous blowlamp paint removal.
- Always strip coatings by hand, and never have the unit 'dipped' in an acid bath for paint removal, as this will destroy any composition decoration, glue will be dissolved, and the entire frame may shrink and twist.

Cast Iron
- If a cast-iron fireplace unit has been restored, make sure this has been done correctly. A usual method is to have a strip of metal (strap) screwed across the back for support, after which the front crack can be welded (a very difficult, specialist, operation).
- Look for corrosion of burner parts, particularly splits and cracks.
- Look at the back – some antiques have stamped registration marks or numbers.
- Antique castings have more delineation and detailing than reproductions.
- Nineteenth-century iron feels lighter than new metal.

Generally
- Beware if something seems very cheap: it could be a poor quality reproduction.
- Always ask if the item is original or reproduction: there are very good reproductions now that are almost indistinguishable from the real thing.
- It's a good thing to find something 'in the paint', as this is evidence of a genuine antique.
- A badly restored fireplace is worth less than an unrestored, incomplete fireplace.
- Get a receipt, stating whether it is original, and its approximate date.
- Take a photo if you are collecting at a later date.
- If an item is incomplete on inspection it's unlikely ever to be complete – don't believe that 'the missing parts are in the other part of the yard'. And it is unlikely you'll ever find suitable spare parts.
- Firebricks are often missing from firebacks, and this is not necessarily a problem, as there are companies making an assortment of firebricks.
- Buying from a specialist will cost more, but you are paying for expert restoration, compatibility with building regulations, and you have redress if there are problems.
- If your building is listed, check with your conservation officer as to whether you are allowed to replace or alter any of the fireplaces.

ABOVE: **Carved wooden chimneypiece with cast-iron fireplace and tiled panels.**
(Courtesy Mongers Architectural Salvage)

LEFT: **Quaint and rare wooden mirrored chimneypiece with cast-iron fireplace with tiled panels, including a hearth.** (Courtesy Mongers Architectural Salvage)

Marble Restoration

Restorers repair marble by replacing areas with matching new material, gluing it in place with coloured resin-based adhesives, and filling or setting in a 'strap' of stainless steel at the back – crack repairs or joint lines are masked by an apparent vein line.

To clean marble, brush away loose dirt from crevices, then wash with warm, soapy distilled water, working from bottom to top to avoid streaks of descending grime. Use a bristle brush for cleaning mouldings, and rinse with clean water; dry afterwards with a cloth. A commercial marble cleaner might be suitable for excessive dirt, but wear protective gloves and eye protection. Be very careful what you use, as you can destroy marble's surface by using an incorrect cleaner: bleach can be particularly harmful.

Deep stains are best removed with a poultice-type stripper, with cellophane wrapped over it to keep it in place for the requisite period. Scrape off the poultice when it has worked – stains should have been 'drawn into it'.

For finishing off, use a marble polish or fine white wax polish, wiping this with a dry cloth to polish it up.

Grates

To brighten up a grate use graphite grate polish, which gives a silver-black finish that's ideal for highlighting decorative details. Apply this with a brush and afterwards polish with a soft cloth. Use a wire brush for removing rust from a cast-iron grate, then use grate polish; alternatively you can use stove paint, which dries to a matt black, and is specially formulated to withstand high temperatures. For renovating polished steel, try using fine wirewool dipped in thin oil, protecting your hands with gloves. Working in the same direction, polish the surface to a bright finish, then dry with a cloth. Clean brass or copper with metal polish.

Tiles

The entire fireplace usually has to be removed to get the tile(s) out – this is only normally practical if you are renovating a fireplace before fitting it. Tiles are fixed from behind and held in place by a metal backing frame, which is held by nuts to lugs set into the back of it. Spray the bolt threads with WD40, allow this to soak in, undo the nuts and remove the frame, then take out any tiles needing replacement or repair. When replacing the tile(s), you need wooden packing pieces to make up the thickness so the tile is pushed right to the front. Finally replace the backing frame, then apply bonding plaster to the tile's back to fix it in place.

Sometimes a tile can be removed and replaced from the front. First cut out the broken tile with a cold chisel, using eye protection. The replacement tile has to be cut down in width slightly to fit – do this with a suitable grinder, removing the same amount from each side so that the design remains central; wear eye protection and gloves as the particles are very sharp and dangerous. Fit the replacement using a piece of tape stuck to the front as a holding device, put bonding plaster on to the back and sides of the tile, and place it in position centrally. Clean off any plaster that oozes on to the surface.

To clean up a removed tile that is to be put back, scrape off any plaster that adheres to the back. You can wash a tile with a solution of detergent in distilled water. If the dirt is more ingrained, use water-soluble paint stripper, but soak the tile in distilled water first, as this may prevent dirt being absorbed into the tile's porous surface. Remove the paint stripper/dirt residue with a wooden or plastic scraper, or a brush. Wash the tile in water.

A broken tile can be stuck together again using epoxy resin (two-part) adhesive, applying strong adhesive tape behind to hold the parts in place until the glue has set. Remove any glue that goes on to the surface with a cloth dampened with methylated spirits. If the joint line is visible, touch this in with enamel paint that matches the rest. For chips and cracks, try mixing epoxy resin with talcum powder, to make a repair paste. Fill the chip or crack overfull, then scrape it back flush with the surface with a knife blade.

Stripping Paint from Wooden
or Cast-iron Chimneypieces

Check whether the paint you're stripping contains lead, using a Nitromors tester. If it does, take suitable precautions. For wood you have to be very careful not to use a chemical which may destroy composition mouldings fixed to it. Use chemical strippers carefully, just on the background. Generally you should always test stripping chemicals on an unobtrusive area first: use a soft (plastic or wood) scraper or stiff brush to remove the solution, and wash carefully afterwards. Gel, paste or poultice strippers work best, and always follow the manufacturer's instructions. Always neutralize chemical strippers, as recommended by makers of the product. To strip paint from cast iron the best method is by shot blasting, but only use a specialist firm.

EXPERT ADVICE

Peter Healy, Secretary, National Fireplace Association

Installation costs of a fireplace are high, as the work has to comply with building regulations, and must be carried out by a HETAS registered engineer for solid fuel (wood or coal products) and/or a Gas Safe registered engineer for gas appliances (CORGI in Northern Ireland, Isle of Man and the Channel Islands). For this reason it is vital to ensure that any fireplace functions properly, as subsequent problems are expensive to rectify. Using a gas fire in an antique fireplace is perfectly acceptable, and a number of firms make gas fires to suit most types of surround.

Ferrous Auger, of LASSCO

Always measure the width of your chimney breast, and never have a mantlepiece that is wider than about ½in (13mm) narrower than the breast width – ideally it should be more like 2½in (60mm) narrower each side. A lot of people come to us with the size of the aperture, but this isn't that important, as it can be made bigger or smaller, whereas the width of the chimney breast cannot be altered. You shouldn't take up the entire width of your chimney breast.

LEFT: **MASCo's large stock of radiators of various sizes and styles.** (Courtesy MASCo Architectural Salvage Yard)

BELOW: **A beautiful old cast-iron radiator covered with rust, ready for renovation. If you buy one in this state, make sure it has been pressure tested.** (Courtesy MASCo Architectural Salvage Yard)

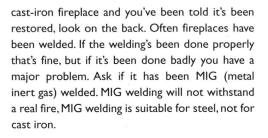

cast-iron fireplace and you've been told it's been restored, look on the back. Often fireplaces have been welded. If the welding's been done properly that's fine, but if it's been done badly you have a major problem. Ask if it has been MIG (metal inert gas) welded. MIG welding will not withstand a real fire, MIG welding is suitable for steel, not for cast iron.

Graham Ball of Robert Agaard

Burnished steel is basically cast iron that goes through various processes on a burnishing wheel. It's a polishing wheel with powders, waxes and so on, the idea being to fill the holes in cast iron, and the speed of the polishing head highlights the metal, you get a finish like shiny steel. Once it's polished it's susceptible to rusting – the atmosphere can make it rusty, even moisture in your fingertips. It needs a regular wipe over with WD40 – this helps to seal it to some extent. For a marble repair it depends what kind of break it is. A clean break can be glued back. Our mason has different colours of epoxy resin-based glues to hide repairs. Sometimes you have to set in pieces of stainless steel in the back to give support – or you can even add extra pieces of marble bonded to the back if there's room.

Neville Griffiths, of Rococo

Don't assume that because you are going to a salvage yard that the cast-iron fireplace you're looking at is an original one. It could be a cheap Chinese import left outside to go rusty. Look at the definition of the casting – for reproductions it's often a heavier casting and the detail is not so precise. The things you should take care to avoid are badly designed wooden fire surrounds. New ones tend to be awful in design. A simple good Victorian fire surround with corbels is always a good buy. Better still if it's got the original surround 'in the paint' – that way you've got more chance of knowing it's an original paint, so it has definitely come from a house. If you're looking at a

RADIATORS

A genuine antique radiator looks far more in keeping with a period room than a bland modern type. This is because the old ones were made of attractively chunky and solid-looking cast iron, and they were larger and more elaborately substantial than the strictly utilitarian, flat panel designs of today. Good reproduction radiators are made, but they are generally more expensive than restored originals. Surprisingly these very early heat transporters are still perfectly serviceable, and can sometimes function better than their modern descendants, being completely compatible with modern heating systems. Being made of cast iron, as opposed to the modern steel, they are therefore heavier, and less prone to rust, but more susceptible to cracks. Original cast-iron radiators convect as well as radiate, meaning they are more efficient than modern ones. The biggest difference between old and new examples is that antique radiators are too heavy to be wall mounted: they were designed to be free-standing, and have their own 'feet'.

Central heating was invented in 1784, when waste heat from factory steam engines was used to power the first steam-fed radiators, and during the 1800s factories and public buildings were heated by these. For most of this period radiators were only used in the type of public buildings where furnaces could be installed. This steam was at an extremely high pressure and colourless, so leaks would cause terrible scalding – high-pressure steam can be 200°C. For this reason steam-fed radiators were abandoned in favour of hot water-fed ones. Churches and stately homes had central heating in the later nineteenth century, and their radiators were ornate and beautiful: indeed some were especially commissioned for a particular building, to match the surrounding architecture.

Around 1890 back boilers were used in large domestic homes, and these could deliver hot water to cast-iron radiators, and were the forerunner of today's central heating. Their use expanded until, by the 1940s, ordinary houses eventually had central heating. Early central heating relied on thermosyphonic principles, and was dependent on wide pipes allowing the free flow of water, on the principle that hot water rises. A thermosyphonic system depends on a sealed system of water, consisting of a number of radiators joined by wide pipes to the boiler's heating chamber. The boiler, ideally at a lower level than the radiators, heats the body of water in its chamber, and this flows along to the radiators, from where the heat is dispersed to the room areas. The water, now cooled down, returns to the boiler to be heated once more.

(Foreground) Various sections of radiators; (behind) underside of an old cast-iron radiator showing its feet. On top are separate feet, and a renovated, newer radiator. (Courtesy MASCo Architectural Salvage Yard)

A radiator on top of two older un-renovated radiators. (Courtesy MASCo Architectural Salvage Yard)

An attractive large cast-iron radiator, already primed and painted. Note the four feet on which it stands. (Courtesy MASCo Architectural Salvage Yard)

Thermosyphonic systems were 'balanced' by a plumber, meaning that instead of selecting a radiator size to match room dimensions, a rough guess as to adequacy was made, then the system 'tweaked' so that individual valves to radiators were partly turned off to restrict the water flow if a radiator was too large for a room. Today it is usual to match the radiator's size precisely to the room's dimensions.

Nowadays all central heating systems rely on a pump to move the water around. The water pressure within the system is consequently higher, and pipes are generally of narrower bore (mostly 15mm). When you switch on the central heating (or the electric timer does so), you are simply operating the pump, which moves the water around. The thermostat in the boiler determines when the boiler cuts in or out. Thermostatic radiator valves – small devices fitted as valves to individual radiators – act by cutting off the water flow once a particular, preset, temperature is reached.

Early radiators were cast in sections that were fitted together. Between each section there was a linking collar with a left-hand and a right-hand thread – the collar turns independently of each section, and there are gaskets (fibre washers) to effect a seal. Radiator colours in Victorian times were bronze/dull gold for churches, dull creams and whites for institutions, and black lead for domestic homes. Only three companies made them, and their names will be found on the top plug. These were Ideal, Crane and ARC (the latter in intertwined letters). Thornton Kay, reclamation expert and proprietor of Salvo, has made a particular study of the functioning of antique radiators, and offers BTU ratings charts for them, allowing you to decide on the optimum size for your room's area. Reproduction radiators are made in the original styles, and the usual pricing rules apply.

Principal Types

- Victorian column radiator (1870 onwards) – squared top and bottom horizontals, joined by columns.
- Patterned (1890s) – one common style was termed 'French Pattern Range'. Comprised of individual vertical columns with raised relief sculptural patterning (for example French freestanding floral, incorporating floral textured designs).
- Neoclassical (1900), featuring square-topped columns (common in schools and hospitals). The first domestic style.
- Princess (1910) with a more rounded top than the neoclassical style that it superseded. First introduced into hospitals because the more rounded style, being easier to clean, was less conducive to the spread of germs.

Practicalities

Cast iron cannot be welded in the ordinary way, as for gas-welding steel. A blacksmith may be able to weld cast iron, but it is a complicated, expensive procedure requiring great skill – which means it is doubly important to check for splits and cracks. Specialists can replace individual sections that are compromised. The fibre washers inserted between component sections may have been damaged.

Buying Tips/Checkpoints

- It is best to buy from a specialist dealer: they will recondition the items before sale and offer a guarantee against leaks.
- One cheaper option is to buy 'tested but unrestored' radiators, that you will have to strip and paint yourself – remember that professional cleaning by shot-blasting might absorb the cost difference.
- If you buy from a general yard not offering a guarantee, always ask if the radiator has been pressure-tested, if it has been stored inside or outside, how long it has been disconnected, and if it has been properly flushed out.

- There are excellent reproduction radiators being made. These are either wall hung or stand on small brackets. A reproduction may also have feet that taper to a point, unlike the genuine antiques, whose feet enlarge at the base.
- Radiators stored outside and lying, stacked, on their sides are likely still to contain water that can cause rust along the seams; also if the water subsequently freezes, and therefore expands, this may cause cracks. Make certain such radiators have been pressure-tested before buying.

RIGHT: **A rare circular radiator.** (Courtesy MASCo Architectural Salvage Yard)

BELOW: **Surface rust on steel radiators, ready for renovation.** (Courtesy MASCo Architectural Salvage Yard)

Miniature quaint un-renovated radiators; notice the small feet. (Courtesy Mongers Architectural Salvage)

Surface paint and rust is best removed by shot-blasting – but stipulate that only fine shot is used, because larger grade shot can cause damage. An alternative method of stripping is by 'dipping' in a caustic soda bath, but not many dealers have the facilities for doing this. You can have them painted or do it yourself using standard oil-based paint, an alternative being to have a 'hand-polished' metallic finish applied, which can be maintained by spraying with WD40 oil and wiping the surface down.

The original valves are not suitable for modern central heating systems because they were made to operate at a much lower pressure, suited only to gravity-fed systems, not the pumped systems of today. But reproduction valves that look the same, but can cope with the pressure, are available, or you can use modern fittings. However, the bushes – the outlets the valves fit into – need to be reduced from their larger size to accommodate modern fittings. There were also 'feeds' at the top corners, which are redundant and need to be capped off. If you have 'Fernox' type additives to the water in your system, make sure these are compatible with raw cast iron, as some of these chemicals could have deleterious effects.

It can be a good idea to use a strong wall-retaining bracket as additional support for the weight, and bear in mind that the floor where you site them needs to be robust enough to support the radiator's weight – around 90lb (40kg). The correct size for your room depends on factors such as the operating temperature of your boiler, speed of the pump, colour of the radiator and its surface finish, as well as the room's dimensions. The correct size can be calculated using Thornton Kay's charts (contact Salvo www.salvo.co.uk).

EXPERT ADVICE

Thornton Kay, of Salvo

The heat from a radiator is a combination of radiant (direct) heat and convected (caused by circulating air) heat. The style, colour and surface finish of a cast-iron radiator affect the proportions of each type of heat given off. A matt-black finish gives out the most radiant heat (the best kind), whilst a white or chrome shiny finish gives the

least. If you're arranging your own stripping, remember that an inexperienced bead blaster can blow holes in the metal, or destroy the fibre washers' seal sections. If you're buying radiators from a heating system that was left undrained in a building during a cold winter, the water in them may have frozen, expanding and possibly cracking the castings.

Andy Triplow, of The Old Radiator Company and Architectural Treasures

Splits can be invisible, and they're not necessarily at the seams, they can crack across the surface and be impossible to see – that's why it's essential for radiators to be pressure-tested. Don't listen if a dealer says, 'This one's a good size': this is meaningless if it bears no relation to your room's actual dimensions. Low-height radiators are worth more than tall ones, because people always want to fit them underneath windows. It's not feasible to refurbish old steel radiators, the cast-iron ones are the only ones worth doing, and make sure the seller can guarantee it before you buy. However, don't be scared of buying an old radiator. Modern radiators are of poor quality, and you could be buying the same radiator as your neighbour, whereas original radiators are sometimes a one-off.

John Bodrell, of The Cast Iron Reclamation Company

The radiators that were made for churches and stately homes are some of the most ornate and beautifully cast iron that you are ever likely to find. Often some of these radiators were especially commissioned for a particular building, designed to match the surrounding architecture. Some of the earliest radiators were tubular with square columned lids or vertical supports. These were often patterned. Church radiators also often carry lattice-top lids that reflect the old floor grates that carried the feed pipes. In the latter part of the 1800s patterned radiators became versatile in the form of individual columns; these were mass produced from one or two particular designs, the most common being the 'French pattern range'.

FLAGSTONES

Paved flooring was once a luxury for the rich only, but became ubiquitous at around the beginning of the eighteenth century. Stone paving was mostly used in peasants' homes, or in the service areas of bigger houses. Initially flagstones were laid on an earth floor on a bed of coarse sand or ash; this inevitably resulted in dampness, the ground's water rising up through the stone to its upper surface. Flagstones can be used inside or outside – generally thinner stones are most suitable for interiors, as less floor excavation will be needed. One advantage of using reclaimed flagstones is the pleasantly worn finish (patina) they are likely to have. Limestone flagstones are particularly suitable for kitchens.

Flagstones, or flags, were made from sedimentary rocks that split readily along the planes of natural bedding. The different kinds are York (buff, grey, brown or bronze), Purbeck (off-white) and Pennant (grey). 'Street' flags, made from dismantled pavements, are usually of good quality sandstone. Locally sourced stone is best, since this blends in better with the building materials of your house. Flagstones are usually laid in even rows, termed

'coursed' work, so you need a constant width; lengths are normally random. Widths can vary from 18–36in (455–915mm), and are sorted into batches of stones of the same width; however the standard course widths are 18, 21 and 24in (455, 535 and 610mm). Thickness can be between 1–4in (25–100mm). Stones that are thinner than 1in (25mm) are best avoided, since they could be salvaged roof tiles; at the other end of the scale don't buy flags thicker than 3in (75mm), as these are likely to be too weighty for safe handling.

New flagstones are being imported from India, but these do not have the characteristics of old

A thin flagstone – always ask if flagstones are genuine old stones, or newly imported from India. (Courtesy Abbots Bridge Home & Garden Renovation Centre)

A pallet of thin flags. (Courtesy Abbots Bridge Home & Garden Renovation Centre)

ABOVE: **Giant sandstone flags, some with a painted surface – remember painted flags can be hard to clean back to their original state.** (Courtesy LASSCO Ltd)

BELOW: **Broken flags, suitable for crazy paving.** (Courtesy LASSCO Ltd)

flags, so if you buy these they should be much cheaper than original antique examples. Prices vary so much that it is impossible to make comparisons.

'Crazy paving' means broken flagstones, made of either stone or concrete.

Buying Tips/Checkpoints

- Don't buy any flags with paint, oil, varnish or mortar staining on them.
- Ensure stones are genuine second-hand ones, and not Indian imports.
- Don't buy flagstones thinner than 1in (25mm) or thicker than 3in (75mm).
- Look specifically for flaking, delamination (where the component layers are coming apart) and missing corners.
- Make sure that the roughness or relative smoothness is compatible with where you want to use them.
- Remember that the thicker the flag, the less material you'll get, as generally you buy by the tonne.
- Check that the flags are not tapered or otherwise not rectangular.
- Beware of flags from old woollen mills, which may have lanolin or oil on the surface, as this may have penetrated inside; any oil inside may seep out over time and be slippery and look unpleasant.

EXPERT ADVICE

David Kirk, Dorset Reclamation

For inside, choose smooth stones that have great natural wear, and rougher-surfaced ones for exteriors. Lamination is a common fault to look out for – it's caused by water trapped within the dismantled floor.

Peter Randle, Ace reclamation

You can use flags internally or externally, but for inside it's generally better to use thinner ones, as this means you don't have to excavate the floor so deeply.

TERRACOTTA FLOOR TILES

Also known as quarry tiles, terracotta floor tiling became practical and popular in the past in areas where stone was not easily available and a hard-wearing floor was needed. Older tiles were larger and thicker than newer ones, up to 12in (305mm) square and 1½in (39mm) thick. They are yellow or red and made of kiln-fired unglazed clay. Normally square, a side of 6in (150mm) was the most usual,

but as stated already, they can be as large as 12in (305mm) square, and hexagonal or octagonal shapes are also available. The thickness varies between ½in (12mm) and 1½in (37mm), the thickest being of the best quality.

Generally they are for interior use, mainly in kitchens and hallways, and are often laid in staggered, brick-style courses instead of the usual grid formation popular today. If you do use them outside, make sure they are frostproof. In the Gothic revival movement, Victorian tile-makers resurrected the method of making inlaid clay floor tiles

ABOVE: **A single quarry tile, to show the surface blemishes, which are a part of their charm.** (Courtesy Abbots Bridge Home & Garden Renovation Centre)

RIGHT: **Thick red terracotta, or quarry, tiles. Their thickness indicates they are old.** (Courtesy Abbots Bridge Home & Garden Renovation Centre)

115

ABOVE: **Excellent grained white marble flooring panels.** (Courtesy MASCo Architectural Salvage Yard)

TOP: **Beautiful grained marble flooring panels.**
(Courtesy LASSCO Ltd)

LEFT: **Lovely hexagonal terracotta floor tiles – notice the varying shades of red/pink.**
(Courtesy Mongers Architectural Salvage)

of differing colours and patterns, often laid with plain ones (geometrics), and these were known as encaustic tiles. Mosaic tiles were made to a predetermined design, which could often be intricate and attractive. Encaustic tiles rarely survive, however, so are not generally available second-hand, though they are now being manufactured in the original way by at least one of the original makers – Minton Hollins.

Buying Tips/Checkpoints

- Check for extreme soiling, limewash or paint staining. Dirt can be removed but limewash and paint cannot easily be taken off.
- Look for flaking, cracking or other damage.
- Inspect for adhering mortar, especially at edges: cement mortars sometimes used for fixing them are hard to remove.
- Ensure you see the actual tiles you are getting – they can vary from batch to batch.
- Thicker tiles tend to be older, and also better quality than the thinner modern varieties.

EXPERT ADVICE

Alan Berks, of Opus Property Services

Wear and tear imparts charm, as does a less-than-pristine surface. I've always thought that part of the charm of a reclaimed tile is you don't want it to be particularly clean, otherwise it may as well be new. The aim in fitting a reclaimed tiled floor in an old house is that people assume it's the original floor. There will often be all sorts of shades and textures within a set of tiles and in various 'through traffic' areas, meaning some will be worn and misshapen, or even holed. Avoid these, or arrange them so they're under kitchen units.

David Kirk, Dorset Reclamation

Avoid tiles that have cement mortar adhering – these will have been laid on a cement screed and they just don't clean up very well, and grinding away the mortar is very time-consuming.

Safety and Flagstones

- Handling a dead weight such as a flagstone can damage your back. Bend your knees and keep your back straight when lifting. Wearing a lumbar belt support can be a good idea, especially if you've had back trouble in the past.
- Wear gloves.
- Wear goggles, a mask and thick gloves when cutting stone with an angle grinder.

Practicalities for Flagstones and Quarry Tiles

Cleaning

- To clean a flagstone floor or flags themselves, you can try scrubbing with washing soda diluted in water, or for heavier stains caustic soda (one tablespoon in 5ltr/9 pints of water), but protect your eyes and hands in case of splashes.
- For even heavier staining, pour on solvent stripper and spread it around leaving it as thick as possible, then rinse and scrub with hot soapy water, using a scrubbing brush and sponge, again taking care to protect yourself from splashes.
- Mildew or mould should be treated with dilute household bleach or a biocide.
- For cleaning quarry tiles or tiled floors, try light scrubbing, pressure-washing or using a brick-cleaning chemical. Don't use sandblasting, as this will remove the tiles' attractive patina of age, along with the dirt.
- Do not use scouring powder, metal scourers or wire brush on tiles.

Cutting Flagstones

Use an angle grinder with a suitable disc (wear eye and face protection and gloves). In theory you can cut flagstones with a hammer and chisel, but this takes much practice.

Cutting Quarry Tiles

If they are not too thick, you can use a heavy duty tile-cutting jig – DIY stores sell inferior quality ones for cutting wall tiles, but these are totally useless for thicker tiles. Alternatively use an angle grinder to cut them (using safety protection).

Finishing

Do not seal or varnish a quarry-tiled floor, as this will seal dampness inside, and may also make them dangerously slippery. In fact it's unnecessary to seal them at all, but if you want to apply wax polish, then a suitable choice is Johnson Traffic Wax. Apply it to a dry, dust-free surface and follow the manufacturer's instructions. Note that all polishes will darken the surface, possibly enriching the natural colour.

It is usually unwise to seal a flagstone floor, as this can create a slippery surface, and/or seal in dampness, which could lead to structural breakdown.

Replacing/ Resetting a Flagstone

If a flagstone is worn down disproportionately to the rest, the best approach is to raise it and re-lay it on a thicker mortar bed, perhaps turning it over if the underside is better than the top side. Take great care, as it's easy to chip, crack or break the stone.

- Chip away the surrounding mortar, then insert a crowbar or large screwdriver to lever it upwards. If you're raising an entire floor of flags, the hardest stone to remove will be the first.
- The new flagstone may have tapered edges; if so, you should make the top surface the large one, as the angle is designed to lock the pointing mortar in place and to make a more secure fixing.
- Make a bedding mortar mix of one part cement to three parts of sand and add a small amount of water so the mix isn't too wet – a guide is to squeeze the mortar, and if it retains its compacted shape, that means the water content is right; if it crumbles apart add more water.
- Wet the sub floor lightly, then put in the bedding mix and re-lay the stone. Tap it down very gently so it is flush with the rest, using a rubber mallet or a large piece of timber to spread the force of a wooden mallet's blows.
- Use a similar 1:3, fairly dry mix to point in the

joints around the edges – you may need to use pigment in the cement so as to match the remainder of the pointing, in which case use white cement (Snocrete).

- Fill the joints and tamp down the mixture, using a small piece of plywood on edge, hammered down – keep adding more mortar and tamping until the joint is flush.
- Then brush away the top surface so the mortar is just below the face of the stone: do your best to avoid staining the stone surface with the mortar, as will inevitably happen if the pointing mix is too wet.

Replacing/Resetting a Quarry Tile

- Wearing suitable eye and hand protection, smash out the damaged tile using a club hammer and cold chisel, working from the centre outwards.
- Once removed, dig out about ¼in depth underneath to make room for the cement-based tile adhesive. Wet the recess, then coat the back of the new tile with adhesive.
- Place it in position so it is central, with even gaps around the edges, and carefully tap down.
- Then grout the gaps, using cement-based grouting.

SETTS

These are man-made cubic stones, for use as a floor covering. You can sometimes find fine collections of these in salvage yards.

Setts, for paving floors. (Courtesy Abbots Bridge Home & Garden Renovation Centre)

CHAPTER 7

Baths, Basins, Taps and Wooden Staircase Parts

BATHS, BASINS AND TAPS

Because good quality old baths were made from cast iron, the thickness and relative resistance to corrosion of this metal means that even centuries of rust can be cleaned away without adversely compromising the structure. What is more, there are now excellent new enamelling techniques that can make a second-hand bath as good as new.

Somewhat rarely for second-hand building items, it's not feasible to buy a decrepit old bath and renovate it yourself. Several companies specialize in selling second-hand baths that they have professionally renovated, and offer a guarantee with these. Unfortunately this means they are rela-

tively expensive, on a par with new baths, however these products are genuine antiques and are guaranteed to have a long life. Second-hand steel baths might be available, but they hold no particular historical appeal, and are only likely to be worth acquiring if you happen to find one in good condition that's appreciably cheaper than something new. It's very easy to tell a steel bath from a cast-iron one: the latter is incredibly heavy, while the former can be carried easily by a single person.

Second-hand taps are sold either fully restored and guaranteed by specialist dealers, and are accordingly costly, or are offered 'as seen' with no guarantee, very cheaply. Renovating some parts of a tap (see below) is fairly straightforward, but only

Selection of old basins and loos.
(Courtesy Cox's Architectural Salvage Yard)

119

LEFT: **Pedestal basins and baths at MASCo's showroom.** (Courtesy MASCo Architectural Salvage Yard)

BELOW: **Large attractive cast-iron bath with bulbous feet.** (Courtesy Mongers Architectural Salvage

ABOVE: **Large 'plunger' cast-iron bath with plain feet.** (Courtesy Cox's Architectural Salvage Yard)

RIGHT: **Close-up to show a 'plunger' mechanism – it says 'Waste' on the release knob.** (Courtesy Cox's Architectural Salvage Yard)

BELOW: **Grand old baths big enough for two – or even three!** (Courtesy MASCo Architectural Salvage Yard)

a specialist can do major repairs, and they will charge a lot. So buying an untested tap can be a worthwhile gamble.

Most professional bath restorers also produce reproduction taps, and sometimes other reproduction items as an adjunct to selling the restored originals. These are often made in the same way as the originals, as is the case with Thomas Crapper Ltd, so if you fit this type of high quality reproduction taps to a genuine antique bath, you won't be compromising its appearance.

TOP RIGHT: **MASCo's fine range of brass, nickel and steel taps.** (Courtesy MASCo Architectural Salvage Yard)

MIDDLE RIGHT: **Brass bath tap set and waste, still in the box – a real collector's item.** (Courtesy MASCo Architectural Salvage Yard)

BOTTOM RIGHT: **An old-style wooden washstand with marble top.** (Courtesy Heritage Reclamations)

BELOW: **Rare brown earthenware 'butler'-type sink.** (Courtesy Cox's Architectural Salvage Yard)

Older basins and WCs are made of earthenware. Cracks or crazing in this material means they will leak. However, more modern porcelain examples can have cracks in their surface but remain watertight. Basins and WCs are not complicated and fit the old computer maxim, 'What you see is what you get'. Quite a number of beautifully decorated ceramic Victorian WCs are still around.

1930s-style pedestal basins, loos and so on.
(Courtesy Heritage Reclamations)

Masses of bathroom basins at MASCo's.
(Courtesy MASCo Architectural Salvage Yard)

Glossary

bateau or chariot bath Rises up at both ends. French in origin, normally about 5ft (1½m) long, very deep and usually footless.

bath/shower mixer Originating in the 1920s, this features a lever that diverts the water from bath to shower; some had a 'telephone'-style handset. These are very complex mechanically.

canopy bath The most luxurious type of all, incorporating a shower enclosure; the canopy, or hood, contained taps from which fine jets of water would flow.

double-ender/baignoire French style, with semi-circular ends, a central waste and taps, and generally 3–5in (75–125mm) deeper than British roll-top baths.

ears The four spokes on a tap handle.

feet The four floor-touching metal shapes fixed to the bath's base. They were usually bolted to lugs fixed to the bath's shell, and came in various styles, including ball-and-claw and square.

gland A tap's mechanical part, encompassing the washer enclosure, which presses against the pipe's end to block water.

globe taps Non-spouted tap for roll-top baths (originally Victorian) requiring a hole in the bath's vertical wall.

head/handle (for tap) Typically the 'capstan' style with four 'ears'.

index/indices The ceramic lettered part(s) in the centre of the tap's head.

parallel-sided bath The same width all the way along.

plunger bath Usually British, this utilizes the eponymous tubular plunger device.

plunger A rod or tube fitted to a bath internally or externally, incorporating a lifting knob to activate the waste plug.

roll-top baths The description pertains to the bath's rim; those with feet came in a variety of different types.

shield Domed cover concealing the tap's mechanism.

slipper bath Rises up at only one end.

spindle Central shaft on a tap, operated by the handle that goes up and down, thereby applying pressure to the water-closing washer.

swan neck Where a tap's upper part replicates a swan (eighteenth/nineteenth centuries).

tapering bath Narrower at its tap end, wider at the bottom end.

ABOVE: Cast-iron bath prior to renovation – plenty of rust, and the enamel is damaged too. (Courtesy LASSCO Ltd)

TOP RIGHT: Eclectic range of beautiful old cast-iron baths at Mongers. (Courtesy Mongers Architectural Salvage)

RIGHT: Close-up of a bath foot – make sure you have all four when you buy, as replacing one is virtually impossible. (Courtesy Mongers Architectural Salvage)

LEFT: Early cast-iron bath in need of care and attention. (Courtesy MASCo Architectural Salvage Yard)

BOTTOM LEFT: The crazing on this basin doesn't matter – it should still be perfectly watertight. (Courtesy MASCo Architectural Salvage Yard)

BELOW: Range of butler's sinks. (Courtesy MASCo Architectural Salvage Yard)

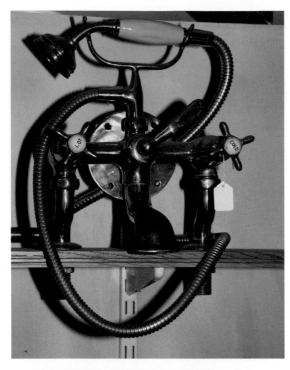

Elderly 'telephone'-style brass shower/mixer tap. (Courtesy MASCo Architectural Salvage Yard)

Later chrome finish, 'telephone'-style shower/ mixer with shower attachment missing – always check that such items are complete.
(Courtesy MASCo Architectural Salvage Yard)

ABOVE: **1884 design toilet-roll holder.**
(Courtesy MASCo Architectural Salvage Yard)

OPPOSITE TOP: **1930s-style angular taps, nickel plated.** (Courtesy MASCo Architectural Salvage Yard)

OPPOSITE BOTTOM: **Another early telephone-style shower/mixer, with porcelain handles and insets.** (Courtesy MASCo Architectural Salvage Yard)

Old timber-seated loo by Shanks of Glasgow. The instruction says 'To use urinal lift the seat'.
(Courtesy Heritage Reclamations)

WCs, LOOS OR LAVATORIES

Sir John Harrington is reputed to have invented the first flushing water closet in Queen Elizabeth I's reign, but this device was only installed in the grandest houses. Joseph Bramah's valve closet was invented in 1778, following a patent lodged by Cummings in 1775. This incorporated an earthenware pan fitted with a trap that opened when a handle was pushed, coinciding with the release of water from a cistern above the bowl. Then the brilliant engineer Thomas Crapper further improved the WC mechanism by inventing the ballcock, the valve device still used today, whereby a hollow ball

Very early brass shower/mixer tap. (Courtesy MASCo Architectural Salvage Yard)

Timeline

Pre-Victorian	The earliest baths were portable, made from zinc, fireclay or copper. They had to be filled with water from the kitchen range, meaning hot water had to be carried upstairs. The fixed baths that came later were of fireclay or cast iron coated with vitreous enamel, or even wood, lined with copper.
1820s	Cast-iron mains and steam pumping engines for water delivery meant that for the first time water had sufficient pressure to be piped into tanks in house attics, permitting plumbed-in bathroom fittings.
1840s	The idea of a bathroom evolved from the practice of fitting the bedroom of a large house with a WC, bath and basin. Ceramic baths were the earliest type.
1837–1901	Taps were brass or nickel-plated with china indices and flat profile ears, with a large gland nut on the body. Globe taps were invented. Spouts elongated progressively throughout this era.
1850s	Cast-iron roll-tops were first invented, but were not in common use until later. Basins were supported by brackets on the wall or elaborate legs. Pedestals came later.
1860s	Purpose-built bathrooms on the first floor became a feature of the finest homes. A terraced house frequently had a bathroom in a rear first-floor extension and a separate WC in an adjacent room.
1880	Cast-iron roll-tops were becoming more popular.
1918	Baths became less elaborate, adapting to the new straitened circumstances of post-war Britain, where there were many fewer large houses with servants. These utilitarian shapes set the trend for baths today.
1920s	A nickel-plated finish began to replace brass for taps, and a domed shield covered the interior, making the tap's body more rounded. Convex ears were popular. Art Deco taps were mostly angular and multifaceted, featuring hexagons, squares and octagons. The bath shower mixer with hand-spray arrived.
1930s–1960s	Chromium-plated finishes replaced nickel-plated, and simple rounded shapes were popular.

ABOVE: **Old cast-iron high-level cistern.**
(Courtesy MASCo Architectural Salvage Yard)

RIGHT: **Beautiful floral design on this Victorian loo.** (Courtesy Mongers Architectural Salvage)

(originally metal, now plastic) on an arm rises with the water level in the cistern, thus closing the inlet when the correct level is reached. His nephew, George Crapper, improved the syphon mechanism by which water flow is initiated.

It is very sad that Thomas Crapper, this great plumbing engineer who gave us such a splendid invention, should be forever associated with a crude reference to a bodily function: in fact it is claimed that the reference is actually related to a Dutch word Krappe, and Thomas's relevance is coincidental. Most late Victorian houses had a Crapper WC with a high-level cistern, and we are still using Thomas Crapper's technology in modern WCs. His factory, along with its original name, has passed into the hands of an excellent company who are still making WCs, basins and baths in precisely the same way they were made then, and they, at least, are giving him the respect this great man deserves.

Sadly, very few original WCs survive from a demolished building. Twycliffe is one of the names to look out for. Beautiful artistic designs were often fired into these lovely old porcelain pans.

Buying Tips/Checkpoints

Restored Taps
- Only buy from a specialist dealer.
- Ensure they have been pressure-tested, guaranteed and fitted with adaptors to be compatible with modern plumbing systems. You may need to add valves to make them comply with water by-laws.
- A pointer to genuine authenticity is the metal: old brass is of a different, more coppery colour than the new material, which is of a more yellow hue, the latter indicating a reproduction. Reproduction taps are also often plated in gold, which can look brash.

Non-Restored Taps
- Turn the spindle and check that it stops and doesn't continue to spin – the latter indicates that the metal threads have worn.
- Don't pay too much, as complete restoration may be needed.
- Check that replacement taps comply with water by-laws – you may need to add valves.
- Check the metal for authenticity: old brass is of a different colour than new (see above).
- Don't economize on your waste fittings. A genuine Victorian/Edwardian waste has a cross-shaped grid and a finely detailed chain-stay.
- Check the external appearance: indices can seldom be replaced or repaired, and professional replating costs a lot.
- Refurbishing old taps by changing washers is a relatively easy DIY job, but those with serious faults require expensive professional engineering attention.
- Adaptors are available for making old fittings compatible with modern plumbing systems.

Baths
- If possible, buy from a specialist bath renovator, who'll offer a choice of items that are guaranteed.
- Check plunger mechanisms, as these cannot be repaired. They must be complete and working.
- Check for corrosion, especially around the waste.
- Make sure your bath is as complete as possible. A missing foot can be impossible or expensive to match, as can absent taps and waste fittings.
- Ensure fittings are compatible with modern pipework.
- Be certain that your floor can support the great weight of a cast-iron bath: you may have to ensure that there are supportive floor joists directly beneath the site, as floorboards alone will not be sufficiently strong.
- Antique bathroom basins and WCs should be checked for cracks, crazing or breaks in the glazing finish (for earthenware this is irreparable, but porcelain items may still prove to be watertight).
- If you buy a bath with taps already fitted, make sure these work before having the bath plumbed in.

EXPERT QUOTES

Simon Kirby, of Thomas Crapper Ltd

An old loo with a beautiful floral design can obviously look extremely attractive, but bear in mind that for evermore the rest of your bathroom is going to have to match that colour scheme. Many people admire our old loos, but end up buying a plain white one for this reason. We have fifty or a hundred old decorated loos here, just for display. In addition we have for sale about a dozen such pans that have been fully tested and are guaranteed for use. If you buy from a reputable dealer, they should guarantee that an old pan is serviceable, and you have recourse to take it back if it is not.

It is very important to understand that old loos were designed to be used with either low-level or high-level cisterns, and only an expert knows which is which: a high-level cistern used incorrectly can cause splashing and flooding, whereas a low-level cistern used inappropriately won't have sufficient water pressure to flush properly. It's vital to check that your old lavatory doesn't leak – a common fault. Flush pipes linking cistern to pan are also crucial and must be of the right diameter. Remember that unlike a basin or bath, a WC has to contain water permanently, so a fault in the glazing can mean leaking water and a useless loo – once water comes through it just keeps dripping.

Old WCs were made of earthenware, which is not intrinsically waterproof – it relies on the waterproof glaze on its surface. So any flaws in this glaze, for example crazing, will allow water to seep in and it will find its way out somewhere else, usually through the foot. Over a period of time, the floor can get damp and smelly! Often these cracks in the glaze are so tiny you can't see them.

We put in a professional 'bung' (blocking device) in our antique WC pans, and fill them above the waterline with water and leave them for three months: it really can take this length of time for a leak to become apparent. Only after this test do we guarantee the loo against leaking. Connections for the waste to soil pipe are usually no problem – a plumber should be able to marry them up to modern soil pipes, except in a few cases; also water connections to old cisterns are the same as modern ones – they haven't changed in a century. And if you love the look of an old loo but it's not suitable to use for its original purpose, it can make an absolutely splendid flowerpot!

Practicalities

Baths

Originally metal baths were coated in vitreous enamel and fired to 1100°C in a factory kiln, using materials that would breach permitted safety standards today. Nowadays professional bath restorers use a process whereby the old surface is removed via shot-blasting, then the inside resurfaced using secret methods, but which are basically the application of compounds such as epoxy resins and/or enamel paints. The outside is primed and painted. The factory-produced protective surface is always guaranteed, and it's important to go to a company that is old established, otherwise its guarantee may be valueless. Bathshield have a trademarked process that was developed in Switzerland twenty years ago and has been improved ever since, involving the material being finally baked on, using infrared lamps. Antique Baths of Ivybridge use a twelve-stage restoration process with an epoxy primer, enamel midcoats and a polyurethane-based topcoat, which is finally sanded and polished. There are various DIY products, but reports concerning their longevity and quality are mixed.

Feet came in a range of shapes and sizes, including ball-and-claw, square, cubed and rounded, meaning that matching missing ones is not easy. Specialists usually keep a stock of random spares for matching, or can even cast another (usually from aluminium – in appearance similar to cast iron), but this is expensive.

Taps

The professional restoration process comprises cleaning the exterior of putty and other adherents, using a wire brush or scraping. Then the item is stripped down to components, cleaning out packing from the packing glands, removing limescale from surfaces, and making any new parts required. Exterior parts may be re-plated. Then the tap is reseated, whereby a new mating surface is created on the perimeter of the tap's central waterway, so that the rubber washer meets it squarely. Finally a new packing gland washer is fitted, and the tap reassembled. When dismantling, you will find that the head is mounted on to a square peg at the spindle's top, and this can be very hard to remove. The internal mechanism of ordinary taps is fairly simplistic, but threads and sizes differ widely and are not usually interchangeable – there are many different sizes of thread, and specialist parts have to be made. Bath/shower mixers are extremely complicated.

DIY restoration can include polishing the exterior with chrome cleaner and removing limescale with limescale remover, lemon juice or vinegar. Re-washering involves the reasonably straightforward process of dismantling the tap and removing the old washer and replacing it with a new one. A DIY tap-reseating tool is available, but is not likely to be as effective as the equipment used by professionals.

EXPERT QUOTES

Simon Kirby, of Thomas Crapper Ltd

Taps shouldn't be an afterthought. I think of taps and wastes as bathroom jewellery, because fine examples enhance the whole room, whereas inappropriate or unauthentic brassware can spoil the whole effect. Either buy fully restored and guaranteed taps from a specialist, or do your own rudimentary checks, buy cheap and take a chance.

Martin Chadder, of Bathshield

I love the longevity of baths. On a recent television programme they sent a submarine into the wreck of the Titanic, and I saw a sensational plunger bath in the Captain's quarters. Even after nearly a century, two miles under the sea, I know that I could restore that bath to perfection.

Thornton Kay

Earthenware is a porous material which relies on a vitreous glaze to make it impervious, so an early Victorian cracked or crazed old earthenware WC pan or basin is likely to leak. From the later Victorian period onwards most sanitaryware was made from a stoneware which is impervious, so damaged glazing is less important. It's a good idea to look for basins with the taps still attached. Get your plumber to check that the taps work before a sink or bath is fitted. One way of cleaning an old bath is to apply neat cream cleaner, leave this to soak for a day, then rub with a green polypropylene scourer and water. Old bath enamel can be resurfaced, but old, slightly less glossy enamel is actually safer than high gloss for babies and old people.

WOODEN STAIRCASE PARTS

It's pleasant to imagine replacing your entire staircase with a magnificent ornate example from a grand house, but it's usually impractical to do so. This is because a staircase is a three-dimensional object which performs a function. So you have to make sure that the rise, width and depth, the way it is 'handed', and how it meets the landing on the next floor, plus other variables, meet your building's exact requirements. So if you are considering the possibility of fitting an entire staircase into a house you will definitely need the skills of an architect or master carpenter, who'll be able to tell you whether your chosen staircase will work in your house or not, and it's extremely unlikely that it will. Alternatively, if you happen to find a magnificent antique staircase you can insert it into a house that's at the planning stage, so the building can be designed around the staircase, rather than the other way round.

Set of old turned balusters/spindles, with squared sections top and bottom, with mortise cut-outs to facilitate fixing. (Courtesy Cox's Architectural Salvage Yard)

Set of spindles with interesting shaped cross-section. One of them has its timber stripped back to the wood, whilst the rest are stained and varnished. (Courtesy Cox's Architectural Salvage Yard)

Four different heights of spindle.
(Courtesy Cox's Architectural Salvage Yard)

Grand newel post with raised surface designs and a fancy carved head.
(Courtesy Cox's Architectural Salvage Yard)

However, replacing sections of such a structure, either for repair or to add glamour, is relatively straightforward and second-hand parts are quite easy to find. Building regulations pertain to all new installations and replacements, but not to repairs; these state that the minimum handrail height is 35½in (900mm), and no balustrade opening should allow for the passage of a 4in (100mm) sphere. If your home is listed you will need listed building consent for any changes.

These structures were usually either painted to conceal a variety of different timbers, or the softwood parts were stained and/or grained to simulate darker hardwoods.

When planning to alter, replace or tinker with your staircase, remember that you must not cut corners, because safety has to be a number one priority. The Royal Society for the Prevention of Accidents (ROSPA) reports that trips, slips and falls down stairs are among the most common accidents in the home, with children up to four years old being the most potentially vulnerable. And anyone over seventy-five who has a staircase accident is more likely to have a fracture than a younger person, something that can potentially be fatal for those in that age category. Consider a handrail that is bonded merely by inadequate adhesive to a newel post, when a screw or dowel attachment is absolutely vital: this appalling bodge could mean that someone elderly, who trusts to a handrail's integrity more than most, would be very likely to hurtle into space without warning. The

designer Laura Ashley and the legendary folk singer Sandy Denny both died in their prime as a result of falling down stairs.

Many people cannot accept that the speculative building of the late eighteenth and nineteenth centuries tended to be common work, or carpentry that was plain rather than sophisticated. They mistakenly replace the original ordinary rectangular balusters with incompatible, elaborately carved and turned spindles that would never originally have been used.

Second-hand newels and handrails can be very expensive, but are far more attractive than newly made ones. Old staircase spindles, if in good condition, are about four times the price of new spindles that are available in builders' merchants (for example the fine Richard Burbridge range). Even though new staircase parts can be extremely attractive, the timber from which they are made cannot have the patina of age.

TOP LEFT: **Three different handrails.**
(Courtesy Cox's Architectural Salvage Yard)

BOTTOM LEFT: **Several sets of spindles.**
(Courtesy Abbots Bridge Home & Garden Renovation Centre)

BELOW: **Section of balustrade.**
(Courtesy Cox's Architectural Salvage Yard)

Glossary

baluster or spindle Turned or square-section timber rails, or decorative black-painted iron uprights.

balustrade Complete section, comprising balusters, handrail and newel posts.

barley sugar twist Description of a particular kind of timber shaping, where the shaft has been carved so that it resembles a twist of barley sugar.

blocks Diminutive, rough-timber square-section blocks, glued underneath steps to strengthen the right-angled joint between tread and riser.

carriage Centrally placed beam that supports a wider-than-average staircase from underneath.

curtail step Bottom step of a flight that has a curved semi-circular end.

going The total depth of a stair's tread from front to back, minus the projection of one nosing.

handing Refers to the position of the balustrade relative to the walls.

handing, handed Refers to the side where the handrail is positioned, that is for right- or left-hand use.

handrail Continuous rail for hand-gripping, often elliptically shaped, and often made from a hardwood such as mahogany. Balusters are fixed to its underside.

newel/newel post Chunky, elaborately carved or turned post at the bottom, or at turns, in a flight of stairs, fixed to both the bottom stair and the handrail.

nosing Small outcrop of the tread that projects beyond the riser – it is often a separate piece of moulding.

overall rise The total height that the staircase needs to bridge.

pitch The angle between the floor and the stair line.

reverse nosing Separately applied nosing fixed to the side of treads in an open-tread construction.

rise Height of the stair riser.

riser Vertical component of a step.

scotia moulding Concave moulding that is sometimes pinned on the riser beneath the nosing.

spandrel panel Triangular-shaped panel that fits under the outside stringer and fills the space between the string and the floor below.

splat balusters Type of early timber baluster shaped from flat pieces.

step Made from two boards, the tread and the riser.

string or stringer Panel that covers the side of a flight of stairs. It usually incorporates housings (cut-outs) to receive the edges of treads and risers.

swan neck/knee-and-ramp Shaped sections of handrail joining straight sections at changes of level between flights.

tread Horizontal component of a step.

volute, cushion or snail Spiral-shaped section at the lower end of the handrail.

wedges Small, tapered, rough chunks of wood that are hammered into the tread-to-string housing joints to take up any slack.

winders Diagonally shaped steps that join two sections of straight flights.

Types of Staircase

Cantilevered: Where stairs are fixed to the wall on one side, but unsupported on the other. More usual for stone staircases.

Closed string: Construction type where the string hides the treads.

Open, or cut string: Construction type where the sides of the treads are visible above the string.

Dogleg: Flight of stairs with a 180-degree turn at a half landing.

Geometric: A cantilevered staircase, its side string winding up around an open well, without newel posts.

Mast newel staircase: Spiral staircase with a central newel that rises up through the building.

Open well: Where two flights that turn as a dogleg are separated to give a spacious effect. Their straight connecting section is called a quarter landing.

Timeline

Medieval	Wooden ladders outside or inside buildings. Stone spirals within grand houses and castles.
14th and 15th centuries	Mast newel (spiral, with a central pole) stone and timber staircases in vogue. Alternatively solid wooden blocks were laid against an internal wall.
1590s to early 1600s	Framed stairs with separate treads and risers replaced earlier, more simplistic designs: characteristics of the period were closed strings, heavy balusters and short flights of oak steps. Richer homes might have balusters and newel posts featuring acorns and heraldic devices. Handrails and strings were made of impressively carved oak. Dogleg turns arrived, as did open-well staircases.
17th century	Newel posts had ornamental finials, heraldic beasts being popular in grand houses. Non-tapering balusters or splat balusters were common. Staircases were becoming more refined, with more sophisticated handrail designs. Late in this century, square-panelled newel posts with flat newel caps became widespread. Balusters were large, elaborate and vase-shaped.
18th century	The cut-string staircase was invented, largely superseding the closed string. A classical influence made stairs less chunky. Newel posts were less functional, and balusters were lighter, vase-shaped and fluted. The barley sugar twist for balusters became popular, and scrolled brackets decorated open-string panels; reverse nosing was applied to tread sides. Wrought-iron balusters were becoming progressively simpler and thinner. Regency staircases had slim, square iron balusters, with narrower handrails that continued over the top of the newel, frequently finishing with a scroll or a wreath.
1750–1800	Oak was used less, handrails and newels were often mahogany, and everything else was made of painted pine. Dogleg staircases were common in small homes, arriving in larger houses by the end of this century.
1790s	Solid square-panelled newels with flat caps were typical.
1700–1900	Cottages and farmhouses normally had cramped flights of straight steps and winders boxed off against a wall.
1800–1840s	Designs became less chunky, newels less functional, and balusters were fluted and vase-shaped or had a barley sugar twist.
Victorian period	Closed-string staircases were very rare, replaced by the open-string. Balusters were usually square-section wooden bars – two or three per stair, according to the status of the house. The acorn motif was revived for newel posts. Detailed Victorian pattern books, such as *Riddle's Master Carpenter* and those by Abraham Swann, detailed a huge range of staircase designs from which speculative builders could choose.
Late 19th century	The Arts and Crafts movement reintroduced the traditional, more impressive pre-Victorian styles; also oak was reintroduced.

Practicalities – How a Staircase Fits Together

Balusters

In a closed-string staircase balusters are either nailed to the handrail's underside and the string's top edge, or are slotted into place. To replace a jointed one, saw away the damaged original and fix a shortened replacement with screws. For open-string staircases, balusters are housed into the treads; removal of the nosing may expose the joint, then you can prise the baluster out sideways. A split baluster may be repaired *in situ* by prising apart the split and squeezing in PVA wood adhesive, then holding the joint closed, using G-clamps.

Newel Posts

Newel posts are nailed to the floorboards, and also sometimes to the joist beneath. The string and handrail fit into slots cut into the newels, and they are sometimes pegged or screwed into place. To dismantle this kind of joint, identify the fixing by examining the newel's surface for a timber infill: this may be either a fixing dowel's end or timber concealing a screw head, the removal of which releases the timber.

Handrails

For a straight run between newels, this is likely to be screwed through the newel; as with newels, examine the post's surface for a timber infill piece, and remove this to expose the screw for dismantling. Sections making up a length of handrail were usually butted against one another and drawn together there by means of an internal nut winding on threading protruding from the adjacent section. If the nut(s) have worked loose it may be possible to tighten them, but damage to the timber is a possibility. One of the nuts that winds along this length of threading is circular and serrated, so it can be tightened with a screwdriver inserted through a slot in the underside of the handrail; this slot is covered by a piece of veneer, whose colour difference may be apparent.

Treads

Remove wedges from underneath, as well as any Scotia moulding if this is present. Withdraw any visible screws and nails, or else insert a hacksaw blade between tread and riser, and cut through their shanks. If the tread is fixed to the riser by means of a tongue-and-grooved joint, cut through this parallel with the base of the tread, using a panel saw, pad saw or jigsaw. For an open-string staircase remove the return nosing, tap out the balusters and knock out the tread from underneath so it emerges at the front. For a closed-string staircase, break the back joint first, then tap the tread from the front to remove it from behind. Replace the tread with a piece of timber of the same dimensions.

Nosings

If there is Scotia moulding beneath the nosing, remove this first and replace it afterwards. Cut out the damaged section, angling the cuts towards the centre, then replace the missing piece with a larger sized length of suitable moulding. Glue this new piece in place, in addition screwing it, countersinking the screws. When the adhesive has set, plane the timber that stands proud to match the rest, and fill any depressions with wood filler.

Stripping Paint

Softwood items can be 'dipped' in a caustic bath by professional strippers, however this process is unsuitable for hardwood, such as might be used for newels and handrails.

Repairing Creaks

It's not really practical to cure these unless you have access to the underside of the staircase. If so, first try to find where the creaks occur and chalk-mark these areas. Riser-to-tread joints may be to blame: insert screws from underneath to pull them together. Also check that the triangular timber blocks, glued beneath the stairs at the riser-to-tread right angle, have not become partly detached; if so, remove them, sand off the old adhesive and glue them back in place. Finally, check for missing or loose wedges, replacing or refitting as necessary.

EXPERT QUOTES

Thornton Kay, of Salvo

Old second-hand pine staircases are made of better quality timber than those available today. Prior to 1700 balusters were usually turned using English unseasoned or green oak, and these are identifiable because the round timber becomes slightly oval in cross section due to unequal shrinkage across the grain. Newel posts do not necessarily have to match the rest of the staircase.

Peter Watson, of Cox's Architectural Salvage

If you're buying a complete set of balustrading, make sure the seller guarantees completeness, or tells you what's missing. Never buy a speculative pile of bits. Second-hand newels will have had lots of slots cut into them to accommodate floorboards, strings and handrails, so make sure your newel matches the rest of the staircase parts you're buying. If you're buying a newel on its own, be prepared to fill in their slots, which are unlikely to match up with your timbers. If you're replacing several balusters, it may be worth lifting the handrail rather than sawing them off individually, such as you would do for a single replacement. Search out the different coloured 'filling' piece of wood in the newel, remove this and you'll find a screw or a peg – unscrew or knock out the peg. Then you can pull the newel forwards to release the handrail. Then you can ease the handrail off the spindles. Once their top end is free you can ease each one out of its socket in the stringer. If you've got balusters missing or you can't match them with second-hand replacements, you can always get copies made by a good carpenter. But when you take one to be copied, always remove the paint, otherwise the dimensions won't be correct.

CHAPTER 8

Garden Items

GATES AND RAILINGS

Gates and railings were made from one of three types of metal: wrought iron, cast iron or steel. The two types of iron are collectable, but generally speaking steel is not, which is why it is vital to distinguish between the three. Of these, wrought iron was the finest, used mainly to make these items during the seventeenth and eighteenth centuries. It was malleable enough to be worked into many different elaborate forms. Rectangular or square bars were connected by joints more familiar with carpenters – mortise and tenon, halving and pinning –

in order to create the main structure of a gate or railing. It was then embellished by decorative additions such as leaf and scroll shapes, fixed on by heat or forge welding. Finishes might be coloured painting or gilding, not the black that is usual today.

The earliest iron gates and railings in front of London houses (called palisades) date from the 1680s or 1690s, and are of wrought iron. Good examples are the gates to the Fountain Garden at Hampton Court by Jean Tijou, dated 1693. But the usual pattern for eighteenth-century wrought-iron railings is plain bars set into a stone plinth and supported by a top rail, ornamentation being

Railings with hooped tops. (Courtesy Abbots Bridge Home & Garden Renovation Centre)

restricted to urn finials. The main characteristics of early Georgian cast-iron railings are heavy uprights with spiked heads, arrows, javelins or weapon heads.

Georgian gates were normally more simple and graceful than Victorian ones, which had decorative embellishments. From the mid-1800s they began to be made of cast, not wrought, iron.

Cast iron was used in mass production, and entire estates had railings, balconies and verandas made, thus creating characteristic features of the place as a whole, either designed by the architect or selected from a pattern book such as Cottingham's *The Smith and Founder's Director* (1824). One notable Cottingham design was the 'heart and honeysuckle'.

It is worth getting gates with initials or coats of arms, or even emblazoned with a house name, because such gates were invariably of high quality, and you can easily have the inscription taken off. Check that the width of the gate allows access for all the vehicles you are ever likely to need. Gates can also be too large – for instance carriage-drive gates are much too big for most modern homes. Victorian and Edwardian gates usually have rust or damage, but missing parts can be replaced and rust

TOP LEFT: **Gates with arched top finish.** (Courtesy Abbots Bridge Home & Garden Renovation Centre)

BOTTOM LEFT: **Several steel gates.** (Courtesy Cox's Architectural Salvage Yard)

Attractive steel gates. (Courtesy Cox's Architectural Salvage Yard)

Magnificent cast-iron gates and posts. (Courtesy MASCo Architectural Salvage Yard)

Fantastic set of cast-iron gates. (Courtesy Mongers Architectural Salvage)

Close-up of finials. (Courtesy Abbots Bridge Home & Garden Renovation Centre)

can be easily removed. Old gates should be cleaned, painted with zinc-based primer, and then finished with suitable oil-based paint. Gates and railings frequently rot at their base.

In the early eighteenth century only large estates had wrought-iron gates and railings, but in the 1760s cast iron was invented, allowing more intricate designs. Well known cast-iron manufacturers were Macfarlane, Carron and Coalbrookdale. After 1918, mild steel superseded both types of iron for most purposes; during World War II the majority of town railings were sacrificed for the war effort.

Cast-iron units were created in sections, and afterwards these were bolted or riveted together like a form of kit, allowing you to add to width or height. Typical wrought-iron railings have three or four flat horizontals and a round bar at the top, with round vertical bars going through them. Town railings frequently had decorative 'heads', such as spearheads, while country railings were often hooped in pairs at the top.

Gates were normally comprised of a rectangular frame with vertical bars, which are capped in simple finishing finials, such as a spearhead design.

Spearhead finials on a short section of railings. (Courtesy MASCo Architectural Salvage Yard)

Sections of railings complete with concrete base, into which they are set.

(Courtesy Abbots Bridge Home & Garden Renovation Centre)

Glossary

cleave joints Refers to the intricate carpentry-style joints on wrought ironwork.

cross sections Wrought iron normally has a square section, whereas cast iron is either round or square in section, and bars are occasionally fluted.

estate railings Vertical posts are flat-section wrought iron, there are three or four flat horizontals of smaller gauge, and these have holes through which the round bars go, their ends spiked into the ground. There is a round horizontal bar at the top.

fettling The hand process whereby flash lines and faults are removed after cast iron is broken fresh from the mould.

hand melled Fashioned by a blacksmith – this usually refers to wrought iron.

heads or finials The decorative top parts of railings. Examples are spear (cast iron), foliate, obelisk or flattened spearheads. Some sit directly on the top rail as opposed to being fixed to the bars.

heel The receptacle on the ground – for instance a hole in a block of stone – that accepts the base of the gate, allowing it to open and close.

pintle The hanging devices at the top and bottom of a gate that is joined to the rest of railings or a masonry pillar, or at the base on the ground. A cylindrical metal insert goes into the ground, into which a vertical post goes. Or it might be a thick metal plate with a hole in it on the ground. Alternatively the gate can be suspended on two hinges, fixed to a post.

standard The vertical railings at the ends and corners of a run of railings. May be of wider section than the vertical bars (railings), with heads frequently more elaborately ornamented with pineapples, urns, acorns, pine cones or necked ball finials.

top rail This horizontal bar is usually flat, sometimes with a slightly cambered upper surface on handrails.

vertical bars The railings.

Timeline	
1700–1800	Only large estates had gates and railings, and these would normally be made of wrought iron, fashioned by hand.
1760	Cast iron was invented, permitting the creation of more intricate decorative designs, and some railings and gates were made of this shortly after that date; however, cast iron was not in common use at this time.
1800–1850	Cast iron generally replaced wrought iron, and for the first time, ordinary homes had such perimeter protection, previously only afforded to the rich. Notable cast-iron manufacturers were MacFarlane, Carron and Coalbrookdale.
1918 onwards	Mild steel superseded cast and wrought iron for general metalwork.
1939–45	The majority of town railings were sacrificed for the war effort.

Hinges are either both fixed to a post, or have one upper of this type, and at the base a cylindrical metal insert that rotates in a hole in the ground.

Second-hand railings and gates are approximately twice the price of new ones, but are likely to be better built and more decorative. New gates and railings will be made of steel, whereas some second-hand ones may be of the much more alluring cast iron, or even wrought iron.

Wrought Iron, Cast Iron and Steel

Generally, wrought iron was used in Georgian times, cast iron was typically Victorian, and steel was universal after 1945. It is normally reasonably easy to distinguish cast iron from either wrought iron or steel, as it is heavier and chunkier. But it can be harder to distinguish between genuine old wrought iron and modern steel reproductions.

Wrought Iron

Wrought-iron techniques came to Britain from Europe in around 450BC. The first method of converting the metal from the ore was called 'direct reduction', whereby iron oxide was heated in contact with carbon (coke or charcoal) so that the carbon and the oxygen of the ore combined, to leave the metal. The process was performed in small furnaces called 'bloomeries', a bloom being the small lump of iron produced. After this it was further forged.

In the process known as 'indirect reduction' (invented in 1400), iron ore was smelted in blast furnaces to produce 'pig iron'. These 'pigs' were then converted to wrought iron by 'carburization' – the removal of carbon. Various methods were used, the first large-scale process being to smelt pig iron in a furnace; while it boiled it was worked continuously by a 'paddler', and the impurities, including carbon-based chemicals, bubbled to the surface.

The so-formed metal was formed into balls; the next stage was when these hot balls were hammered with the shingling hammer to expel surplus slag, eventually creating 'blooms' of around 5 × 5 × 36in (126 × 126 × 915mm). The red hot bloom was then passed through rolling mills to be reduced in size, finishing life as a puddled iron bar. Its mechanical strength was low, and improvements in strength and ductility were made by reheating and reworking: this is the origin of the word 'wrought'.

The different grades so produced were called Crown Best, Best Best, Best Best Best and Treble Best, the latter being the finest. The resultant bar could also be rolled into sections – for example rounds, flats, squares, half rounds, angles, tees, bridge rails, pit rails, and so on. By 1800 standard sections were bar iron, angle and T irons, channel iron (half H Iron), rolled girder iron, specials sections (including sash bar beading iron, cross iron, quadrant iron), iron bars, rivet iron, chain iron, horseshoe iron, plate iron, nail iron and coated

TOP: Close-up of fluted spearhead and obelisk finials on cast-iron railings. (Courtesy LASSCO Ltd)

MIDDLE: Small cast-iron gate. (Courtesy MASCo Architectural Salvage Yard)

BOTTOM: Railings to match small cast-iron gate in previous picture. (Courtesy MASCo Architectural Salvage Yard)

iron (coated with tin or lead). The material's quality is variable, and there can be variations in section in early iron that was wrought by hand.

Cast Iron

After its creation in 1760, cast iron's further development began around 1800, when the 'cupola' was invented. This was a small blast furnace used to re-melt pig iron rather than smelting ore. After this, many small foundries were established, where the molten iron could be poured into moulds.

The process of manufacture begins with pattern making, whereby the original item is fashioned from timber, wax, plaster or another metal. Then the mould is made: a damp sand clay mixture called 'green sand' that is packed around the pattern; usually the pattern is divided into two parts, to facilitate packing the sand in two sections. The pattern is removed and a void is created in the sand. Molten metal, melted in a cupola, is poured into this void. Once cool, the casting is broken out of its mould and fettling done – this is the final stage, where any mould lines or flash lines or projections from the pouring gates are removed and the fresh casting is brushed clean. When used for making gates or railings, the cast sections are usually bolted together: suitable holes are present in the casting.

Steel

Steel, first known as carbon steel or carburized iron, was made next: this was done basically either by modifying the wrought-iron bloom in the furnace so it retained some carbon, or by heating bloomery iron on a charcoal bed, so that carbon

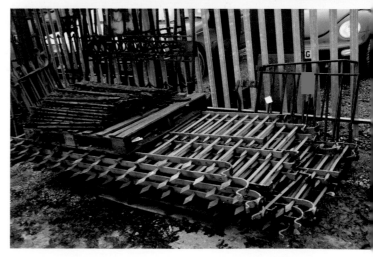

143

ABOVE: **Cast-iron gates – notice the light primer evident where the paint is chipped.**
(Courtesy Mongers Architectural Salvage)

LEFT: **Fine section of cast-iron railings hidden behind a rusty item.**
(Courtesy Mongers Architectural Salvage)

The Three Metals Distinguished

Cast Iron
- Usually has a large cross-sectional girth.
- Patterns appear repeated symmetrically.
- A mould line or flashing, or seams along the edges of bars, may be apparent.
- Sections are never welded together, they are always bolted or riveted.
- The exposed surface may exhibit blow holes and casting flaws, and a fractured surface reveals a crystalline structure.
- The surface is rock hard, and cannot be carved with a sharp chisel.
- Is normally a dark lead-like colour, and cleans to a sparkling brightness. Tiny holes may be in evidence.

Wrought Iron
- Joins were either riveted or forge-welded, or metal 'straps' may be used.
- Examine the welds – forge welding – fire welding – is practically invisible, as opposed to 'puddled' metal, indicating modern gas welding on steel.
- Joints are similar to carpentry joints.
- May have a rolled, hand-beaten or knobbly surface, hammer marks and irregularities.
- Is likely to have a variable girth and cross-section in accordance with the variations of handmade items.
- You can carve away the top surface with a sharp knife.

Steel
- Judge the apparent age of the item – steel was not commonly used until about 1880.
- Joints have modern friction-grip bolts, or fusion (neat and unobtrusive) welding.
- The dimensions of the girth and cross-section are uniform.
- The surface is smooth.

was added to its outer surface, the metal heated to red heat, then quenched in cold water (hardening and tempering – a process impossible to do with wrought iron). Various other industrial processes were developed to create steel in different ways, the most successful being the Bessemer Process (1856). The last forge to make wrought iron in Britain was the Atlas Forge of Thomas Walmsley, in Bolton, which closed in 1973.

Practicalities

Removing Paintwork

If paintwork is not too rusty, sandblasting is the best treatment, otherwise wire brushing. The metal should then be painted with two coats of metal primer (zinc-phosphate-based primers are ideal), then with an oil-based undercoat, finally applying a paint such as Hammerite. If you are removing paint yourself, remember there may be lead-based paint present, so check with the Nitromors test kit, available from DIY stores. If lead is present, either have the paint professionally removed, or take great care to only use wet sanding methods (so as to avoid creating breathable dust), or use chemical paint strippers – the latter with great care and observing all safety precautions for when dealing with old lead-paint coatings.

You are aiming to remove old paint that is not adhering, rust, loose mill scale (this is a substance formed as a result of the hot rolling of iron and steel) and soluble corrosive salts. For sound paint surfaces, your aim is to remove any residual gloss, surface deposits and lumps. If an area is chipped, rub this down too, but ensure that the paint surface under which corrosion may have spread is also cleaned.

Maintaining Paintwork

For ironwork it is vital for paintwork to be continuous to be effective, because corrosion begins at breaks in the paint's surface, then spreads underneath it. Ideally iron paintwork should be maintained every year. Never paint over rust. Ironwork coated with many layers of paint may lose some detail, and in such cases it may be wise to remove it and start again.

Buying Tips/Checkpoints

- There'll always be some corrosion, but check how bad it is. This is likely to be worst at ground level.
- Gates: check for integrity specifically at the hinges and hanging points, where stress and cracks are likely to occur.
- Steel is relatively light, wrought iron is heavier, and cast iron is heavier than both.
- Assess which of the three metals it is, by looking at the features of each (see above).
- Scrolled decoration: in wrought iron the central curl is curved and slightly flattened, however in steel the curl is straight and uniform. Scrolls in cast iron are precisely curved and of regular thickness.
- Cast iron's painted surface can conceal splits and repairs, so check carefully for these, and for hairline cracks. Note that some cracks in decorative parts can be repaired, but damage to structural parts cannot.

Re-setting Ironwork into Masonry

If you are re-setting ironwork into masonry, this has to be cleaned and treated carefully; if it is corroded too badly, a blacksmith may be able to re-tip the ends with stainless steel or an alternative metal, for the distance of the housing plus a minimum of $\frac{1}{2}$in (12mm) from the masonry face. Some recommend fixing it in place using lead or leadwool packing.

EXPERT ADVICE

Peter Watson, of Cox's Architectural Salvage

Do not buy a cast-iron gate if it is broken in a structural part, as any repair is not likely to last; however a crack in decoration can be brazed and painted afterwards. For wrought iron, or even steel railings, you may pick up a bargain if you are prepared to take bent or broken railings and have them repaired by a blacksmith. A gate complete with its original posts is a good buy. My favourite gates are the Victorian cast-iron ones, where they ran riot with all sorts of decorations. Purists would probably go for the earlier gates, say Georgian wrought-iron ones. But for sheer flamboyance and decoration you can't beat the Victorians. The great problem with cast iron is its tremendous weight and brittleness – if you drop one, it just breaks. If you see obvious welded joints, the item is likely to be modern; if it's riveted it is more likely to be older. A red-hot rivet goes through the hole, then it's beaten so the metal spreads, and when cool, grips.

Clive Wilson, of WRS

For gates, check the hanging points especially, for that's where all the stress is. Sadly 90 per cent of the railings sacrificed for the war effort were never used. For anything in cast iron, usually over a period of time you'll find there's a breakage, something has snapped. For example, look at a row of finials: there'll probably be one missing, and the exposed surface will be uneven with obvious air holes, and pitted. Georgian and earlier wrought-iron railings were hand-melled by a blacksmith in

the fire. They would heat up the bottom rail, then drive a hand-held wedge or chisel through the metal into a swage block (block of metal with a specific-sized hole in it) underneath. Then they would insert the end of a heated upright railing into this hole, turn it over and hammer the protruding end part flat, so that, like a rivet, the metal flattened and expanded within the hole, bonding it firmly to the rail – that's a fire weld. They would fix the railing to the bottom rail like that, then make a series of holes in the top rail and fit this to the top of the railings, holding them in place with little iron wedges. Alternatively, some railings might have a thread on the top end.

Finally, above the top bar you might attach heads as decoration, for instance metal shaped into *fleur de lys* shapes, either screwed on to the thread, if present, or heated and melled on. To spot a hand-melled piece of metal you're looking for differences in it. For example, if they made a gate square section or oblong, the only way was to heat and draw it out and beat it in the heat, to make it square or round. It won't be regular, you'll have hammer marks. There are still skilled blacksmiths who can do this kind of work.

Garden seat with cast-iron legs and support and timber slat seating. When timber slats rot these can easily be replaced.
(Courtesy MASCo Architectural Salvage Yard)

146

METAL AND TIMBER GARDEN SEATS AND TABLES

RIGHT: **Metal garden bench seat.** (Courtesy LASSCO Ltd)

BELOW: **Another cast-iron bench seat.** (Courtesy MASCo Architectural Salvage Yard)

LEFT: **Cast-iron garden bench seat with an elaborate design in the casting.** (Courtesy LASSCO Ltd)

BELOW: **'Pub' table. The heavy central shaft keeps it stable.** (Courtesy Heritage Reclamations)

Cast-iron garden seating was generally made up of two metal side panels, also sometimes a metallic back, with timber seating slats bolted on to these. The timber part is, of course, prone to rot, but is easily replaceable. Several British foundries made cast-iron seating, the most famous being Coalbrookdale, Falkirk and Carron, and a famous French manufacturer was Val d'Osne. The various styles are referred to by the patterns on the panel; the earliest Coalbrookdale design was 'Convolvulus', dated 1860. Most of them were made between 1850 and 1910, with modern reproductions, copied in China and Europe from originals, dating from 1970. The original sand-cast pieces were properly fettled, so won't display flash lines; however, modern repros are not so well finished off, so marks and lines like this are a sign of a reproduction.

'Pub' tables – typically having three splayed and decorated cast-iron legs with a pierced iron or wooden top – were of many designs, the most common being the 'Britannia' pattern, displaying Britannia's mask on the shoulder of each cabriole (meaning 'shaped') leg. The wooden tables in public

TOP: **Three-legged pub table with detailed design on the cast-iron legs and a timber top.** (Courtesy Heritage Reclamations)

BOTTOM: **'Pub' table, dainty and graceful, made in cast iron.** (Courtesy LASSCO Ltd)

Buying Tips/Checkpoints

- An original Coalbrookdale seat will have domed brass nuts on the sides to hold it together.
- Aluminium, often used to mimic cast iron, is much lighter than the latter. It won't be attracted by a magnet, as iron will.
- Tiny air holes on the surface (blow holes) and flaws, flash lines and cavities indicate a crudely finished modern reproduction.
- Rust on a modern piece will be a bright chemical orange colour.
- Check for rotten and ill-fitting wooden slats.
- Most cast-iron parts will be painted, which can conceal evidence, repairs or inferior castings: examine the surface carefully for raised, repaired areas or hairline cracks.
- Check for corrosion around bolt holes
- On a genuine piece you'll find rust in crevices, not as a generalized coating.

houses were replaced in the nineteenth century with cast-iron ones; these were heavy enough to stand their ground, and will not easily tip up.

Coalbrookdale

The Coalbrookdale Foundry began producing iron items in 1709, and was run by Abraham Darby, then by his descendants throughout the 1700s. They began by making domestic items and engineering castings, first producing iron rails in 1769. In 1799 the famous 'Iron Bridge' was made.

Garden furniture in cast iron began being made in the early 1800s: seats, plant stands, urns, fountains, gates and railings. Interestingly, most of the Coalbrookdale designs tend to be based on foliage of different kinds: Fern and Blackberry, Lily of the Valley, Nasturtium, Passionflower, Oak and Ivy, and so on. Eminent sculptors of the day, John Bell and Christopher Dresser, were commissioned to make unique designs. In 1851 Coalbrookdale exhibited at the Great Exhibition, and in 1875 published a large illustrated catalogue amongst which was a Garden and Park Embellishments section. The company is still making copies of its original designs in cast iron, and also a range of these in aluminium.

STONE AND TIMBER SEATING

The Romans introduced marble benches, and before 1800, marble, timber or stone was the only kind of outdoor seating. Marble seats were also imported from Italy when the rich began travelling on the continent. In fact before the eighteenth century, garden furniture was only used in affluent homes. The majority of English stone seats were of Portland or Bath stone, made in slot-together sections, the majority of styles being ecclesiastical: one such is the 'Holy Sofa' (1900), being rustic with Celtic designs. Marble seats (Carrara and Istrian were popular types) frequently featured classical styles with lions and griffin end supports. Edwin Lutyens inspired a type of wooden bench seat with a raised curved back. Another variety was termed 'steamer' furniture because it was used on the decks of open liners. Another wooden type was called 'estate', meaning that it was made by the estate carpenter of a country estate. Very old timber seats are unlikely to have survived, so anything more than around 200 years old is going to be of stone or marble. Copies were sometimes made of composition or cast stone (see below), or may be hand carved.

Wooden garden bench seat. Although the timber is green with lichen, it is perfectly sound.
(Courtesy LASSCO Ltd)

Stone garden seating and table.
(Courtesy LASSCO Ltd)

EXPERT QUOTES

Anthony Reeve, of LASSCO

You can sometimes buy a pair of cast-iron bench 'ends' relatively cheaply, but check that the feet are solid and the bolt holes not rusted through. After you've had the metal sandblasted and painted, fix on suitable wooden slats. Buy garden seating in December, when prices will be lower.

Alex Puddy, of Architectural Heritage

It's fascinating that the factory stamp – or diamond plate – on a genuine Coalbrookdale piece is numbered, so you can trace it back to when the design was first registered. Sadly, of course, a copy might also reproduce this.

Nic McElhatton, Chairman of Christie's, South Kensington

One way of assessing whether or not a cast-iron piece has age or not would be to turn the seat upside down and look at the feet. The underside of a genuine antique seat's feet will have a large area that meets the ground, and this will be glassy smooth and flat. On the new reproduction pieces the underside of the feet tends to be a bit rough, and because is hasn't worn down much, you only get a certain smaller area of wear: the foot is basically uneven, because of the poor quality of the casting. The manufacture of cast-iron wares from companies such as Coalbrookdale is evidenced by the metal's dense glassy nature, signifying the high quality nature of the refined iron used. Later reproductions tend to be cast from inferior, unrefined iron.

ABOVE: **Rare rustic timber bench that looks almost like a living tree.** (Courtesy LASSCO Ltd)

BELOW: **Incredible garden seat, built from stone.**
(Courtesy MASCo Architectural Salvage Yard)

Chris Topp, of Chris Topp

For practical purposes there are two kinds of wrought iron: charcoal iron before the end of the eighteenth century, and puddled iron thereafter. Both are resistant to corrosion because of their impurities of included slags, and of the two, perhaps charcoal iron is the more durable. Puddled iron is more consistent and more of a pleasure for the smith to work.

Rupert Van der Werff, of Summers Place Auctions

Cast iron can be very brittle, similar in that way to porcelain. So if something is dropped or knocked with a heavy object it cracks fairly easily. People tend to like weathering on pieces. To a certain extent moss is worth money – they like things to look as if they've been in the garden a long time. We always advise people not to clean things before bringing them to auction – cleaning will seriously affect the selling price, as it takes many years for the mosses and lichens to return, and people love them. The only things we sometimes clean ourselves are marble figures that have gone black and really gungy, so you can't see the detail. But this has to be done by a professional restorer, it's not an amateur job. Weathered marble is very soft and I've seen some awful things. People might put bleach on the surface, or even attack it with a scrubbing brush! This can wipe out the entire value of the piece.

James Rylands, of Summers Place Auctions

Rust on a modern piece might be a bright chemical orange colour, Italian carved stone attracts moss and lichen within three years, so this kind of weathering is not necessarily an indication of antiquity.

(Centre) **Complete staddle stone** *(left)* **base and** *(right)* **top.** (Courtesy LASSCO Ltd)

ABOVE: **Large staddle stones.**
(Courtesy LASSCO Ltd)

RIGHT: **Small staddle stone.**
(Courtesy LASSCO Ltd)

STADDLE STONES

These were also known as 'mushroom stones' because of their shape. They were originally used to raise tithe barns and granaries, barns and hayricks off the ground, to prevent the building's contents being damaged by damp and attacked by vermin: the mice and rats could not climb around the 'caps' of the staddle stone. Regional differences mean they come in variations of form, shapes of base, and in different types of stone. They are popular as garden ornaments, especially in rural areas. 'Staddle' was the old English word for 'stump', so these supports were probably originally made from tree trunks, until it was discovered that they wore out too quickly.

Staddle stones went into disuse around 1945. West Country stones are traditionally of granite, in the Cotswolds of limestone and Bath stone, in Sussex of Portland stone, and in Cheshire of red sandstone.

EXPERT QUOTES

Peter Watson, Cox's Architectural Antiques:

The prime problem is opportunistic theft. Make sure the top is cemented to the base part, as the two together are normally too heavy to shift. And if possible make sure the base is cemented into your driveway or into the ground. Most antique staddle stones will have chips on the top, because of the way they were used – heavy beams were place on them to support the base of the barn, so they're likely to be knocked about a bit, but this doesn't matter at all. The nice old ones are lichened up, and this is attractive, you should leave it in place. You might find a metal eye fixed into the side, this was for fixing a set of staddle stones together when they supported a building. The majority of tops are mushroom shaped; a few are square, but that's unusual. I've seen some where the top has been turned upside down and hollowed out to form a birdbath. Or the base might be used as a topless table, where pieces of stone are put on to make a table.

Pyramidal bases are the most common. In Sussex you get round ones, and up North they tend to taper downwards. The finish at the top is flat, that is the surface where the mushroom top is placed. Sometimes you'll find a metal spike there to locate in the mushroom above.

Robert Grimond, Woodland Farm

The pyramidal-shaped ones are more valuable than the cone-shaped ones. These are brown in colour and they weather fabulously. Others might be made from clunch – this is a chalky colour, but these are not such high quality as they tend to crumble over time. You're looking for a nice shape with plenty of patina on it. Old moss can look good, too. Some of the limestones weather well; these are greyer stone, they weather and attract lichen.

Ham-stone staddle stones are the best, second most popular are the grey limestones, thirdly the

light brown Forest-of-Dene stones, or Saracen stone, which is light brown or a mixture of greys. Staddle stones vary in height but are normally around 28in (710mm). They're nice to put on a patio to form a table – you can turn the top upside-down to make a table. The Egyptian pyramid one is flat on four sides, and the shape of the cone is like an upside-down ice-cream cornet.

Neville Griffiths, of Rococo

Some of the bases may have stood outside for years without a top – sometimes you can see where water's penetrated down the top of the stone, eventually the stone will split. Be aware of it – there may be a hole that someone's drilled for a metal spike. Make sure the top matches the base you might find a limestone top with a sandstone base, they were often separated. If you've got a nice piece of grass outside your house, staddle stones are a way of preventing people parking on it. Most are used as focal points in the garden – architecturally they're very practical. Sets of staddle stones are more expensive than a single or pairs.

See how chimney pots can complement foliage and greenery? (Courtesy Heritage Reclamations)

Large terracotta chimney pot. (Courtesy Abbots Bridge Home & Garden Renovation Centre)

CHIMNEY POTS

Recent building regulations mean that it's rare for people to install antique pots to fulfil their original function. Instead there are companies that make most of the old styles and shapes, and their products conform to the required safety standards. However, old chimney pots are undeniably beautiful, and their chief function nowadays is for displaying plants in the garden.

Old pots can be cylindrical, octagonal, hexagonal, square or spiralled. The tallest can reach as high as 90in (230cm), weighing 200lb (90kg), though they are usually shorter and around 60–120lb (30–55kg) in weight. There is an amazing variety of styles with astonishing names, made by famous pottery firms such as Doulton and Red Bank Products (the latter is still trading). Most are two-part or one-part constructions, though some of the tallest can be in three parts, comprising base, barrel and top. Originally these were glued together in position with cement, while nowadays epoxy resin is used.

In Elizabethan times, ostentatious, brick-built, multicoloured chimneys were popular as a status symbol, in sculpted and heraldic patterns, spirals, lozenges, chevrons and fleur de lys. By the eighteenth century they blended into a roof as merely functional structures surrounding one or more flues (the passageways that transported smoke and

Assortment of chimney pots.
(Courtesy Cox's Architectural Salvage Yard)

ABOVE: **Various terracotta chimney pots.**
(Courtesy MASCo Architectural Salvage Yard)

RIGHT: **'Bishop's mitre'-shaped chimney pot.**
(Courtesy MASCo Architectural Salvage Yard)

BELOW: **Metal chimney pot.** (Courtesy MASCo
Architectural Salvage Yard)

fumes). However, they really came into their own in Victorian times: a single roof often had a variety of different designs. Typically, pots were mounted on the chimney stacks of the new rows of coal fire-burning terraced houses. Pots became a relatively inexpensive way of extending the chimney's height, though many were subsequently removed due to the advent of central heating. The ornate sections of a pot were made by pressing clay into plaster moulds, and for three-part pots, clients could pick and mix from ranges. Thrown pots – cylindrical-shaped examples, or the central barrel of a more complex design – were turned on the wheel by travelling potters, who produced a number of sections that were subsequently joined, with a bead added on top for strength, prior to kiln firing.

Chimney-pot names

Cylinders Usually with a rolled top, or 'bellied' (tapering in at the top): cannon, beehive, crown, Long Tom, tallboy, Dublin can, four-pocket roll, bishop, captain (large and ornate).

Louvred With curved side vents or horns (down-ward-pointing pipes set into the shaft): three-ring louvre, crown-top louvre, octagon louvre, horned louvre.

Square Ornamental square, plain spiked, moulded square, plain taper, square panelled, panelled spike.

Octagonal Fluted octagon, square-base octagon, ornamental octagon.

Random names Lady Broughton, cannon, three-horned roll.

Checkpoints/Tips

- Cracks – tap the side and listen for a 'hollow' ring.
- Glued repairs – these may be no problem, but you should get a discount.
- Cement on the rim – removing this often causes damage, although old lime mortar residue should scrape away quite easily.

EXPERT QUOTES

Neville Griffiths, of Rococo

Old pots can look great in the garden. I have a pair of old vented pots with candles inside, either side of my French doors for lighting the patio. One customer created a chess set with chimney pots, and actually played the game in his garden! The spiky-topped ones were 'kings', those with an undulating pattern 'queens', domed ones 'bishops' and square castellated ones 'castles', and he used small red pots as pawns. Buff-coloured pots tend to be weaker to the elements. Look for signs of crumbling, caused by acids in the soot. Look for any fresh cracks, which could be indicative of being dropped when taken off the roof. If a part is missing or chipped, you can trail flowers and plants over to conceal it.

Peter Watson of Cox's Architectural Salvage

Make sure it isn't cracked – watch out for hairline cracks especially. Tap it with something metal and see if it's got a ring to it, which will denote that there is no crack. For garden display, cracked ones will eventually fall apart. If this should happen, you can repair the crack with two-pack masonry epoxy resin glue. Pots varied according to area. We're in the Cotswolds, so you'd only tend to get buff-coloured ones around here, whereas in Cheltenham they're all beige. Preston pots tend to be the shiny salt-glazed brown ones. Bishops are square ones with ears on the corner.

STATUARY

Garden statuary – also referred to as 'garden sculpture' – became popular in England after it became fashionable for the upper classes to travel around Europe on what was called 'the Grand Tour'. They were fascinated by the number of antique statues on display there, especially in Italy, and wanted similar items on their own country estates. Italian sculptors carved reproductions of originals in white marble for export to England, which meant that by the early 1700s copies of many of the fine original statues of France and Italy

TOP: **Pig with tusks (stone).** (Courtesy MASCo Architectural Salvage Yard)

BELOW: **Grand stone horse, virtually life size.** (Courtesy MASCo Architectural Salvage Yard)

were in England. These copies were themselves copied.

In the eighteenth and nineteenth centuries statuary was hand carved, unlike more recent ones which are cast and made from composition stone (see below). Generally speaking, people like weathered pieces, and, as with stone seating, moss is worth money. On the whole it is best never to clean or remove moss, lichen or staining, as this adds authenticity and charisma to the piece, and if you remove it, this will definitely detract from its value.

Statue of a youth, possibly in the style of Narcissus. (Courtesy MASCo Architectural Salvage Yard)

Marble

Carved marble pieces do not go back further than the mid-1700s – although they were made before that time, there are hardly any of these left. Even marble can be reproduced in moulds (see below), but most of the original copies of famous statues were carved, and this material is prized above all others for garden statuary. Marble reproduces fine detail more accurately than other stones, and its beauty is unmistakable. Even weathered or damaged marble statues are expensive and desirable. When a fine marble piece is kept indoors, its fine smooth finish is referred to as its 'skin'. In outside conditions, this beautiful surface texture can be lost and the item's finish becomes more like ordinary stone. A good way of judging the quality of a figure is by looking at the quality of carving of the hands and feet.

Stone

Up until 1900 most stone statuary was hand carved, but after this date composition stone was cast into moulds. A large variety of stones were used, all of which weather in different ways. Vicenza stone, soft limestone from the eponymous town in Italy, was used for garden statuary up to and including the twentieth century. This 'ages' very quickly, and its porous surface encourages the growth of lichens and mosses; unfortunately it does not weather well in bad climates.

Terracotta was also used for statues, as well as Coade stone; one notable artist of the period was Blanchard. Check that the outer protective glaze is not eroded – if it is, the piece may be vulnerable to cracking. You can tell very early terracotta by its buff colour. Red-coloured terracottas are normally Victorian.

OPPOSITE: **Obelisk? Folly? Whatever you want to call it, this would enhance any garden.**
(Courtesy MASCo Architectural Salvage Yard)

Impressive entrance, but only if your garden is big enough! (Courtesy MASCo Architectural Salvage Yard)

Metals

Statuary was also made in bronze, lead and cast iron. Bronze acquires a green/blue patina in the open. Bronze reproduction items can be made using bronze powder mixed with resin (see below). Many original bronze pieces were signed, so it's worth looking for a signature. The majority of current lead statuary is twentieth century and unpainted, in contrast to earlier lead items which were painted in garish colours. The majority of cast-iron figures were made in France in the nineteenth century: Val D'Osne and Barbezat were the most famous foundries. A good piece is likely to have a founder's mark on its base. Leading exponents were Cheer and Van Nost, the elder and the younger. Cast-iron items are most valuable if they are produced in a famous foundry, such as Coalbrookdale.

Moulded Statuary Materials

Coade Stone

Coade stone is a warm golden beige colour with a slightly shiny surface, making it impervious to weather, unlike its peer terracotta, whose matt surface can succumb to dampness. This excellent and unique fired material was developed by Mrs Eleanor Coade in 1769, and items made in it are very valuable today. It is made from a fired clay aggregate to a secret formula and used to make architectural features on buildings as well as statuary. It is an artificial stone that can give perfect detail, yet is impervious to the English weather. Early Coade pieces are marked 'Coade Lambeth'; later ones, after 1799, are marked 'Coade and Sealey'. The Coade factory copied antique originals and also classical sculpture, and the great sculptor John Bacon was responsible for much of this.

Lead statue of a shepherdess.
(Courtesy LASSCO Ltd)

Lead statue of lady with a lamb.
(Courtesy LASSCO Ltd)

Composition Stone

This stone was first used in the nineteenth century and is basically a concrete – that is, a mixture of fine stone dust and cement to bind the elements. The items are cast in moulds, either as a 'wet mix', or as a much drier mix, in which case the barely moist mixture is packed hard against the mould's surface. After removal from the mould, the items have to be cleaned up and mould flash lines and similar flaws repaired/removed. These were made using iron armatures for strength, which, if they rust, can cause spalling cracks. Austin and Seeley were famous makers of statuary from artificial stone.

Composition Bronze

Composition bronze is made by mixing bronze powder with resins, which is then packed into a mould; this process is a relatively recent invention. Real bronze is, of course, much more desirable, much older, and generally looks more attractive. If in doubt you can tell if something is made of genuine bronze by tapping it: a real bronze piece will ring, but a resin item will give a dull sound.

Composition Marble

Composition marble is a compound made from ground marble mixed with resin.

A stone eagle that looks as if it is poised for flight.
(Courtesy Abbots Bridge Home & Garden Renovation Centre)

Buying Tips/Checkpoints

- Inspect a figure's hands and feet for faults.
- Cast iron, lead and composition stone items had iron or steel armatures which can corrode and cause cracking – check for rust stains, and cracks.
- Look for wear on one side alone – this shows that a statue has been in one position for years.

- Lead – check for corrosion at the back of legs and ankles.
- Cast iron – look for a foundry mark on the base.
- Moss and lichen can be acquired by a modern repro piece, so do not take this as evidence of authenticity.

Useful Contacts

SALVAGE DEALERS

(S) indicates that the company is a member of Salvo.

The majority of the contacts below have their own websites – simply type the name into an internet search engine. Since many of the postal addresses are farms or rural addresses that are not on mapped roads, it is a waste of space to print them, as they would not appear in conventional maps. Contact companies or visit their websites for location details, or you can put the postcode into your satnav.

Where a company specializes in a particular item, this is mentioned in brackets.

I have assembled all the salvage companies I can find, but apologies for any I may have missed out.

Buckinghamshire, Northamptonshire
D. J. Giles Demolition Contractors, 01494 482396, Stokenchurch, Buckinghamshire HP14 3TT
(S) IBS Reclaim Ltd, 01844 239400, Oakley, Buckinghamshire (Yorkstone paving) HP18 9QQ
(S) P. T. Demolition Ltd, 07702 212960, Buckinghamshire HP19 9PH
(S) Ransfords Reclaimed and Conserved Building Supplies, 01327 705310, Daventry, Northants NN11 8XW
Rococo Architectural Antiques, 07872 822 609, Northampton, Northamptonshire NN7 4PN
(S) Site 77, 01296 631717, Aston Clinton, Buckinghamshire HP22 5EZ

E. G. Swingler and Sons, Bugbrooke, Northampton (01604 833500) (roofing tiles and slates) NN7 3PH

Cambridgeshire
Classic Reclaims Ltd, 01833 270088, Oundle, Peterborough PE8 4PZ
Hive Antiques, 01223 860319, Cambs (tiles for walls, hearths and fireplaces) CB1 2LJ
Popple's Reclaims, 01733 203860, Cambs PE7 1XE
(S) Solopark PLC, 01223 834663, Pampisford, Cambridgeshire (major suppliers, huge stocks of bricks, tiles etc.) CB2 4HB

Devon, Cornwall
(S) Antique Baths of Ivybridge, 01752 698250, Ivybridge, Devon (bathroom equipment) PL21 9DE
E. W. Trading, 01271 831001, Barnstaple, Devon (oak flooring, terracotta floor tiles) EX32 7NZ
Eden Reclamation, 01726 852 700, St Austell, Cornwall PL26 8TX
(S) Fagin Antiques, 01392 882062, Exeter, Devon EX5 4PW
Kenmart Timber, 01626 833564, Bovey Tracey, Devon TQ13 9JJ
Magpies Reclamation, 01208 863 828, Wadebridge, Cornwall PL27 7DA
Reusable Materials, 01548 521278, Totnes, Devon TQ9 7AG
Stax Reclamation, 01752 849111, Saltash, Cornwall PL12 6LD
Tobys Architectural Antiques, 01392 833499, Exeter, Devon EX6 8DZ

Dorset, Somerset, Avon, Wiltshire, Hampshire

(S) Ace Reclamation, 01202 579222. Wimbourne, Dorset BH22 8UB

Arcsal, 01749 838 896, Evercreech, Somerset – phone/internet only

Au Temps Perdu, 0781 693 4483, Bristol BS2 0JY

(S) Bathhouse Restoration, 01225 350877, Bath, Somerset BA2 3QE

(S) Bridgwater Reclamation Ltd, 01278 424636, Bridgwater, Somerset (roof tiles) TA6 5EJ

Castle Reclamation Ltd, 01935 826483, Martock, Somerset TA12 6AE

(S) Chaunceys, 0117 971 3131, Bristol (flooring, floorboards, woodblock flooring) BS2 0UJ

(S) Dorset Reclamation, 01929 472200, Wareham, Dorset BH20 7JZ

(S) Frome Reclamation Ltd, 01373 463919, Frome, Somerset BA11 1RE

Gardenalia, 01225 329949, Bath, Somerset BA1 7JF

Glastonbury Reclamation Ltd, 01458 831122, Glastonbury, Somerset BA6 9LE

Jardinique, 01420 560055, Alton, Hampshire (garden items) GU34 4AP

JAT Environmental Reclamation, 01761 492906, Pensford, Somerset BS39 4JF

(S) Olliff's Architectural Antiques, 07850 235793 & 07712 436588, St Pauls, Bristol BS2 9XZ

(S) Romsey Reclamation, 01794 524174, Romsey, Hampshire SO51 8DU

(S) Rose Green Tiles & Reclamation, 0117 952 0109, Fishponds, Bristol BS5 7UP

Salisbury Demolition Ltd, 01722 743420, Wilton, Wiltshire SP2 0DL

Sanitary Salvage, 01980 863030, Salisbury, Wilts (sanitaryware) SP5 1QA

Semley Reclamation Ltd, 01747 850350, Shaftesbury, Dorset SP7 9AH

(S) Source Antiques Ltd, 01225 469200, Bath, Somerset BA2 4LD

(S) South West Reclamation Ltd, 01278 444141, Bridgwater, Somerset TA6 4AP

Stained Glass Group, 07903 152611, Wells, Somerset (stained glass) BA5 2NH

The Beechfield Reclamation Co. Ltd, 01380 730999, Devizes, Wiltshire SN10 2ET

Wells Reclamation, 01749 677087, Wells, Somerset BA5 1RQ

Gloucestershire, Oxfordshire, Berkshire

Antique and Modern Fireplaces, 01242 255235, Cheltenham, Gloucestershire GL50 2BQ

(S) Architectural Heritage Ltd, 01386 584414, Taddington, Gloucestershire (garden statuary) GL54 5RY

ATC (Gloucester) Ltd, 01242 220536, Cheltenham, Gloucestershire (floors and doors) GL50 2TJ

Burgess & Sons, 01869 346347, Bicester, Oxfordshire OX27 7HT

(S) Cox's Architectural Salvage Yard, 01608 652505, Moreton-in-Marsh, Gloucestershire (vast eclectic range – including probably the largest collection of doors in southern England) GL56 9NQ

J. Brant Reclamation Ltd, 0118 981 3882, Tadley, Berkshire RG7 4RT

(S) LASSCO House & Garden Ltd, 01844 277188, Three Pigeons, Milton Common, Oxfordshire OX9 2JN

(S) Lichen Garden Antiques, 01242 609551, Tetbury, Gloucestershire (statuary, urns, flags, staddle stones) GL8 8AA

(S) Minchinhampton Architectural Salvage Company (MASCo), 01285 760886, Stroud, Gloucestershire GL6 8PE

(S) Oxford Architectural Antiques, 01367 242268, Faringdon, Oxfordshire SN7 7AA

(S) Ronson Reclaim, 01452 387890, Sandhurst, Gloucestershire GL2 9NG

(S) The Original Architectural Antiques Co., 01285 869222, Cirencester, Gloucestershire GL7 5PN

(S) Trainspotters, 01453 756677, Stroud, Gloucestershire GL5 1RN

Upton Original Wood Co., 01235 851866, Didcot, Oxfordshire (flooring/beams) OX11 9HS

(S) Winchcombe Reclamation Ltd, 01242 609564, Cheltenham, Gloucestershire GL54 5NT

Windmill Architectural Salvage Co. Ltd, 01453 833233, Nympsfield, Gloucestershire GL10 3UH

Hertfordshire, Essex, Bedforshire

Adelphi Antiques, 01206 792881, Colchester, Essex (fireplaces/grates – open by appointment only) CO1 2NH

Architectural Antiques, 01234 213131, Bedford, Bedfordshire MK40 3RQ

(S) Architectural Salvage Source, 01727 822986/ 07960 351141, London Colney, Hertfordshire (bricks plus masses of other things) AL2 1BB

(S) Ashwells Recycled Timber Products Ltd, 01375 892576, Upminster, Essex (timber beams, flooring, sleepers) RM14 3TL

Blackheath Demolition and Trading, 01206 794100, Colchester, Essex CO2 8JB

Brondesbury Architectural Ltd, 01923 283400, Chorleywood, Hertfordshire WD3 6EA

(S) Courtyard at Debden Antiques, 01799 543007, Debden, Essex (garden antiques) CB11 3JY

Heritage Reclamation, 01442 219936, Hemel Hempstead, Hertfordshire HP2 4TL

Herts Architectural Salvage, 01727 824111, London Colney, Hertfordshire AL2 1LP

Iron Fireplace Company Ltd, 01702 421930, Rayleigh, Essex (grates and inserts) SS6 8XQ

J. Brant Reclamation, 0118 981 3882, Reading, Berkshire RG7 4RT

Jon Prigmore, 07854 573685, Bedford, Bedfordshire MK44 2NU

(S) Skyline Reclamation, 01923 226726, Watford, Hertfordshire (roof tiles and slates) WD18 0FL

(S) Southern Reclaim Brick Merchants Ltd, 01296 660555, Cheddington, Hertfordshire (bricks, yorkstone, setts, sleepers) TW3 3RJ

The Sleeper People, 01621 843281, Maldon, Essex CM9 4LQ

(S) V. & V. Reclamation, 01992 550941, Hertford, Hertfordshire SG14 2PW

(S) Victorian Wood Works Ltd, 020 8534 1000, Upminster, Essex (flooring timbers, boards, woodblock, parquet etc.) This company uses reclaimed timber to make new flooring products, as well as machining original timbers so they are of a uniform size. They also have a London showroom, see below RM14 3TD

Lancashire, Cheshire

Antique Fireplaces and Ranges, 01829 740936, Chester, Cheshire CH3 3EB

Architectural Salvage Online, 01244 657976, Chester, Cheshire CH1 6BS

Ashley Reclamation, 0161 941 6666, Ashley, Cheshire WA15 0QF

Beeston Reclamation, 01829 260299, Tarporley, Cheshire CW6 9NW

(S) Capital Group (M/cr) Ltd, 0161 799 7555, Little Hulton, Greater Manchester (bricks, setts, cobbles) M38 9ST

(S) Cheshire Demolition & Excavation Contractors Ltd, 01625 424433, Macclesfield, Cheshire SK11 7TT

(S) English Garden Antiques, 0161 928 0854, Bowden, Cheshire (garden antiques, staddle stones etc) WA14 2SF

Floor Reclaim, 0161 776 1044, Manchester (floors) MK44 5LS

(S) In-Situ Manchester, 0161 839 5525, Manchester, Greater Manchester M15 4FY

(S) Manchester Radiators, 0161 839 8316, Manchester, Greater Manchester (radiators) M15 4JW

(S) Nostalgia, 0161 477 7706, Stockport, Cheshire (fireplaces, marble chimneypieces, sanitaryware) SK3 8BH

(S) Pine Supplies, 01204 841416, Bolton, Greater Manchester (timber flooring, beams, skirting, architraving) BL1 7PP

(S) Ribble Reclamation, 01772 794534, Preston, Lancashire PR1 4UJ

(S) Riverside Reclamation, 01204 533141, Bolton, Lancashire (timber beams) BL3 1RP

(S) Steptoe's Yard, 01254 233227, Altham, Lancashire BB5 5TX

(S) Steve Shirley, 01942 867629, Wigan, Lancashire (flags, setts and kerbs) WN2 5DT

Stonescape (UK) Ltd, 01942 866666, Wigan, Lancashire WN3 4NN

The Stonewood Co., 01282 854577, Barnoldswick, Lancashire BB18 5QT

London

Amazing Grates, 020 8883 9590, Finchley, North London (antique fireplaces) N2 8AB

(S) Antique Oak Flooring Co., 020 8347 8222, North London (timber, flooring) N8 7NT

(S) Architectural Forum, 020 7704 0982, North London N1 3AX

(S) Architectural Antiques, 020 8741 7883, West London (fireplaces, mirrors) W6 9NH

(S) Architectural Classics, 020 8144 1377, South West London WC1N 3XX

(S) Drummonds 020 7376 4499, South West London SW3 4HN

Heritage Reclaimed Brick Co., 020 8687 1907, Mitcham, South London (bricks) CR4 4NA

(S) LASSCO Ltd, 020 7394 2100, Brunswick House, South West London SW8 2LG

(S) LASSCO Flooring, 020 7394 8061, East London. SE1 3PA

(S) London Reclaim Brick Merchants, 0208 452 1111 & 0208 452 1124, North West London (bricks) NW10 0EB

(S) Nicholas Gifford-Mead Antiques, 020 7730 6233, South West London (18th and 19th C chimneypieces and garden sculptures) SW1W 8LS

(S) Retrouvius Reclamation and Design, 020 8960 6060, North London NW10 5NR

(S) StoneAge Architectural, 020 8362 1666, Enfield, Middlesex EN2 9BJ

West 7 Reclamation and Flooring Company, 020 8567 6696, Hanwell, London W7 2QA

(S) Westland & Company, 0203 411 9848, East London (chimneypieces, grates, panelling) EC2A 4QX

Midlands, Warwickshire, Leicestershire, Nottinghamshire

(S) Alscot Bathroom Company, 0121 709 1901, Solihull, West Midlands (Victorian/Edwardian/Art Deco sanitaryware) B92 0JB

Britain's Heritage, 0116 251 9592, Leicester, Leicestershire (antique fireplaces – excellent selection) LE1 4LJ

Chase Demolition and Reclamation, 01543 448686, Cannock, West Midlands WS11 9TJ

(S) Conservation Building Products, 01384 569551, Warley, West Midlands B64 5AL

(S) Coventry Demolition Co., 02476 303999, Coventry, West Midlands (bricks) CV8 3ES

(S) Hednesford Reclamation, 0121 502 3920, Wednesbury, West Midlands WS8 7DZ

(S) M. D. S. Ltd, 0121 783 9274, Birmingham, West Midlands B33 8BU

(S) Mark Richens and Sons Architectural Salvage and Reclamation, 01636 893930, Collingham, Nottinghamshire NG23 7NX

(S) Padstow Reclamation, 01902 896219, Wombourne, West Midlands WV5 8AY

Ransfords, 01327 705310, Daventry, Northamptonshire NN11 8EA

Reids Reclamation, 01789 720027 & 07836 505507, Stratford-on-Avon, Warwickshire CV37 8RA

(S) Source 4U Ltd, 07708 023742, Warwick B90 2EL

(S) Thomas Crapper & Co. Ltd, 01789 450522, Stratford on Avon, Warwickshire (sanitaryware, plus excellent reproductions made in the traditional way using original Crapper moulds) CV37 8BL

(S) Warwick Reclamation, 01926 881539, Leamington Spa, Warwickshire CV33 9SA

Warwickshire Reclamation, 01788 522087, Coventry (open by appointment only) CV8 3LR

Warwick Slate and Tile, 01926 612610, Southam, Warwickshire CV47 2RP

Norfolk, Suffolk, Lincolnshire

(S) 3A Roofing Ltd, 01473 730660, Copdock, Suffolk IP8 3JF

(S) Abbots Bridge Home & Garden Renovation Centre, 01284 828081 Bury St Edmunds, Suffolk IP30 0LW

Bakers Timber Ltd (Reclaim), 01485 529 495, Fakenham, Norfolk (timber beams, timber flooring etc) NR21 7QZ

Bulmer Brick and Tile Co., Sudbury, Suffolk, 01787 269232, (makers of bespoke bricks) CO10 7EF

Cobar Services, 01473 658435, Stowmarket, Suffolk IP14 2JA

Heritage Building Supplies, 01502 589111, Lowestoft, Suffolk NR32 2PD

(S) Heritage Reclamations, 01473 748519, Ipswich, Suffolk IP8 3AF

(S) J. M. Reclaim, 01603 881401, Dereham, Norfolk NR20 3JN

(S) Mongers, 01953 851868, Hingham, Norfolk NR9 4AF

Morways Architectural, 01953 483914, Attleborough, Norfolk NR17 1DP

Norfolk Reclaim Ltd, 01485 518846, King's Lynn, Norfolk PE31 8NB

R. & R. Reclamation, 01427 628753, Gainsborough, Lincs DN21 3LQ

(S) Tower Reclaim, 01449 766095, Mendlesham, Suffolk IP14 5NE

(S) Treesave Reclamation Ltd, 01787 227272, Bures, Suffolk CO8 5LD

Scotland, Cumbria, Northumberland

(S) Borders Architectural Antiques, 01668 282475, Wooler, Northumberland NE71 6SN

Cumbria Architectural Salvage, 01697 476420, Carlisle, Cumbria CA5 7DH

Edinburgh Architectural Salvage Yard, 0131 554 7077, Edinburgh, Scotland EH6 5NX

Glasgow Architectural Salvage, 0141 958 1113, Glasgow G14 0AP

Hargreaves, 01324 832200, Airth, Stirlingshire FK2 8LT

(S) Holyrood Architectural Salvage Ltd, 0131 661 9305, Edinburgh, Lothian EH16 4AP

(S) Tradstocks Ltd, 01786 850400, Stirling, Stirlinghire (flags, setts, stone) FK8 3QW

(S) Wilson Reclamation Services Ltd (WRS), 01539 531498, Grange-over-Sands, Cumbria LA11 6JP

Staffordshire, Shropshire, Herefordshire

(S) Blackbrook Antiques Village, 01543 481450, Lichfield, Staffordshire WS14 0PS

Brian Legge Reclaimed, 01885 410579, Hereford, Herefordshire HR7 4NJ

(S) Cawarden Brick & Tile Co. Ltd, 01889 574066, Rugeley, Staffordshire WS15 3HL

Four Oaks Reclamation, 0121 308 0554, Tamworth, Staffordshire B78 3EQ

(S) Gardiners Reclaimed Building Materials, 01782 334532, Stoke-on-Trent, Staffordshire ST4 4LG

(S) Gothic Revival Ltd, 01543 481450 & 07971 295277, Lichfield, Staffordshire (stained glass, Gothic revival furniture) WS15 4PT

(S) Jim Wise Reclamation, 01782 714735 & 01782 790576, Stoke-on-Trent, Staffordshire ST4 7LW

Jura Farm and Garden Antiques, 01886 821261, Worcester WR6 5SF

Keith John Ryan, 01782 283330, Stoke on Trent ST6 2PZ

(S) Leominster Reclamation, 01568 616 205, Leominster, Hereford & Worcestershire HR6 0AB

(S) North Shropshire Reclamation and Antique Salvage, 01939 270719, Shrewsbury, Shropshire SY4 5TD

Posterity, 01531 636380, Ledbury, Herefordshire HR8 1EG

(S) Priors Reclamation, 01746 712450, Ditton Priors, Shropshire WV16 6SS

(S) Rayson Reclamation, 01785 711495, Penkridge, Staffordshire ST19 5RZ

The Victorian Ironmonger, 01588 660157, Craven Arms, Shropshire (Door furniture, fittings) SY7 0HT

(S) UK Architectural Antiques, 07890 728144, Rugeley, Staffordshire WS15 4RU

UK Architectural Heritage, 0845 6449051, Hereford HR2 8EG

(S) Wye Valley Reclamation, 01432 353606, Hereford HR2 6NS

Surrey, Kent

(S) Antique Buildings Ltd, 01483 200477, Godalming, Surrey (oak beams, bricks, barn frames) GU8 4NP

(S) Architectural Stores, 01892 540368, Tunbridge Wells, Kent TN4 9TP

Architectural Treasures, 01233 850082, Tenterden, Kent TN30 6SP

(S) Artisan Oak Ltd, 01223 740140, Molash, Kent CT4 8HN

(S) Bygones Reclamation Canterbury Ltd, 01227 767453, Canterbury, Kent CT4 7BA

Cast Iron Reclamation Co., 020 8977 5977, Little Bookham, Surrey (radiators) KT23 4EF

(S) Catchpole & Rye, 01233 840840, Pluckley, Kent (antique sanitaryware, rolltop baths) TN27 0SA

Comley Lumber Centre, 01252 716882, Farnham, Surrey GU10 4JX

(S) Cronin's Reclamation, 020 8614 4370, Little Bookham, Surrey KT23 4EF

(S) Drummonds Architectural Antiques Ltd, 01428 609444, Hindhead, Surrey GU26 6AB

(S) Esprit du Jardin, 01227 722151, Canterbury, Kent (garden antiques) CT3 1BH

(S) Smiths Architectural Salvage, 020 8393 4139, Epsom, Surrey KT17 3BZ

Sussex Demolition, 01883 626122, Warlingham, Surrey CR6 9SA

(S) Symonds Salvage, 01233 820724, Ashford, Kent TN26 3DD

(S) The Old Radiator Company Ltd, 01233 850082, St Michaels, Kent (radiators) TN30 6SP

(S) Woodlands Farm Nursery & Reclamation, 01483 235536/07774 741321, Guildford, Surrey (flags, bricks, stone) GU3 3DU

Sussex

Ajeer Ltd, 01424 838555, Heathfield TN21 9LL

Antique Chandeliers Ltd, 01342 717836, Copthorne (lighting, chandeliers, etc) RH10 3HX

Architectural Salvage Sussex, 01243 774025, Chichester PO18 0DU

Ashcroft Reclaimed Flooring, 01243 554769, Barnham PO22 0BL

Bathshield, 01342 823243, Forest Row, Sussex (restorers of antique baths) RH18 5EZ

Country Oak, 01273 833869, Hurstpierpoint (oak beams, floorboards) BN6 9EF

Danby, 01892 652883, Crowborough TN6 1TB

(S) Dorton Reclaim, 01444 250330, Burgess Hill RH15 9DG

(S) Ian Kean Ltd, 07738 756891, Hurstpierpoint, (stone garden features, stone flooring – open by appointment) BN6 9EF

The Woodroom, 01825 722260, Uckfield (wood) TN22 3HQ

Traditional Oak & Timber Co., 01825 723648, Lewes (oak beams, doors, flooring) BN8 4EY

Yapton Metal Co., 01243 551359, Arundel (metal items) BN18 0HP

Tyne and Wear

Aladdins Architectural Antiques, 07956 080952, Tyne and Wear (1,500 doors of all sizes and ages, plus fireplaces

G O'Brien & Sons Ltd, 0191 537 4332, East Bolden, Tyne and Wear NE36 0AJ

(S) Olde Worlde Fireplaces, 0191 261 9229, Newcastle-upon-Tyne, Tyne and Wear NE1 4HZ

(S) Shiners of Jesmond, 0191 281 6474, Newcastle-upon-Tyne, Tyne and Wear (fireplaces) NE2 2RA

(S) Shiners Snobs Knobs & Posh Knockers, 0191 2131930, Newcastle-upon-Tyne, Tyne and Wear (door furniture) NE3 2JW

Tynemouth Architectural Salvage, 0191 2966 070, Tynemouth, Tyne and Wear NE30 4AA

Wales and Merseyside

(S) ATC (Monmouthshire) Ltd, 01600 713036, Monmouth, Gwent (doors and floors) NP25 3LX

Cardiff Reclamation, 02920 458995, Cardiff, Wales CF24 5SD

D & P Theodore, 01656 648936, Bridgend, Glamorgan (chimney pots only) F31 3TP

Dyfed Antiques and Architectural Salvage, 01994 419260, Dyfed SA34 0YR

(S) Drew Pritchard Ltd, 01492 580890, Glan Conwy, Gwynedd (antique stained glass plus general salvage) LL28 5TH

Gallop & Rivers, 01873 811084, Crickhowell, Powys, Wales NP8 1SF

J O'Grady Reclaim, 0151 648 6486, Wirral, Merseyside CH61 1DG

(S) R M Rees Contractors Ltd, 01639 711688, Neath, Glamorgan SA11 4DT

(S) Radnedge Architectural Antiques, 01554 755790, Dafen, Carmarthenshire, Dyfed SA14 8LX

Welsh Salvage Company, 01633 212945, Newport, South Wales NP20 2JL

Yorkshire, Lincolnshire, Derbyshire

Robert Aagaard & Co., 01423 864805, Knaresborough, North Yorkshire (fireplaces, marble stone and wood, plus grates) HG5 0JP

(S) Abacus Stone Sales, 07802 982109, Huddersfield, West Yorkshire (flags, slates, walling stone) HD4 5AG

(S) Andy Thornton Ltd, 01422 376000, Halifax, West Yorkshire (panelled rooms) HX4 8AD

Bingley Antiques, 01535 270666, Bingley, West Yorkshire BD13 5AB

Bruce Kilner, 01377 232990, Driffield, East Yorks YO25 8NJ

(S) Chapel House Fireplaces, 01484 682275, Holmfirth, West Yorkshire (fireplaces 1750–1910) HD9 1UH

Gothic Gardens, 01904 656255, York, Yorkshire (Garden items and architectural features – appointment only) YO19 4RW

Hoyland Dismantling Co, 01226 747221, Barnsley, Yorks (timber) S74 0PR

Old Flames, 01347 821188, York, Yorkshire (restored Georgian and Victorian fireplaces) YO61 3HT

Period Pine Doors, 01347 811728/0796 960 7643, Huby, Yorkshire (doors) YO61 1HJ

R. & R. Reclamation, 01427 628753, Gainsborough, Lincolnshire DN21 3LQ

R. F. Landscape Products, 01977 782240, Whitely, Yorkshire (sleepers, setts, cobbles) DN14 0JW

Sheffield Architectural Salvage, 01298 85020, Buxton, Derbyshire (radiators) SK17 9RA

(S) Teesside Architectural Salvage Ltd, 01642 310454, North Yorkshire (door and window furniture) TS7 0BN

Kevin Marshall's Antique Warehouse, 01482 326559, Hull, East Yorkshire HU8 7LG

(S) Viking Reclamation, 01302 835449, Doncaster, South Yorkshire (bricks, oak flooring) DN3 3EE

Whitehouse Antiques, 01347 821479, York, Yorkshire YO61 3NF

Williams Architectural Reclamation, 01427 728685, Doncaster, Yorks DN9 1AQ

USEFUL ORGANIZATIONS

Salvo (www.salvo.co.uk) Useful 'Wants and Offers' section, plus quick links to major salvage dealers, information, publications etc.

Society for the Protection of Ancient Buildings (SPAB), 020 7377 1644 (London). Courses, lectures, technical leaflets, technical advice line (www.spab.org.uk)

National Fireplace Association, 0845 643 1901 (Birmingham). Technical information, leaflets, information.

Victorian Society, 020 8994 1019 (London) Information, advice, lectures, courses (www.victoriansociety.org.uk)

Georgian Group, 0871 750 2936 (London) as above (www.georgiangroup.org.uk)

20th Century Society, 020 7251 8985 (London) as above (www.c20society.org.uk)

Brooking Collection, University of Greenwich, Dartford. At the time of writing this is closed, but hopefully will be open soon.

Weald and Downland Open Air museum, 01243 811363, Chichester, Sussex. Courses and lectures on building crafts, architecture and related subjects (www.wealddown.co.uk)

ARCHITECTS, EXPERTS AND SPECIALIZED CRAFTSPEOPLE/COMPANIES

Ben Sinclair, of Norgrove Studios Ltd, 01527 541545, Redditch, Worcestershire. Specialist glass and leaded light restorer (www.norgrovestudios. co.uk)

Drew Pritchard Ltd, 01492 580890, Glan Conwy, Gwynedd. Dealer in and repairer of antique stained glass – also salvage dealer (www.drewpritchard.co.uk)

Master locksmith, Anthony Jarvis, 07795 598792.

Strippers, 01787 371524, Sudbury, Suffolk. Specialists in supplying materials and offering advice on every kind of paint stripping scenario. Mail order service plus phone advice line (www.stripperspaintremovers.com)

Roger Mears, Conservation Architects, 020 7359 8222 (www.rmears.co.uk) North London. Roger's practice was founded in 1980 and he has built a reputation for sensitive work to a vast number of historic and domestic buildings. He specializes in repairs, alterations and extensions to listed houses, including Tudor House, Cheney Walk and a terrace of Grade 1 listed properties in London, dating from 1658. The company hires out infrared lamps for softening the putty of historic windows.

Julian Owen, Conservation Architect 0115 922 9831 (www.julianowen.co.uk) Beeston, Nottingham. Julian has a vast range of experience with numerous domestic and commercial projects, extensions, alterations, conversions, including the complete restoration of historic buildings. He is also the author of three books for Crowood: *Conservatories: a Complete Guide*; *Kit and Modern Timber Frame Homes*; *The Complete Loft Conversion Book;* and *Home Extension Design* for RIBA.

J. and W. Kirby, 01924 862713, Wakefield, West Yorkshire. Timber frame repair specialists.

Linda Hall, architectural historian (hall.email@virgin.net)

Chris Topp, Chris Topp and Co. Ltd, 01845 501415, Thirsk, North Yorkshire. Expert on iron.

Bulmer Brick and Tile Co., 01787 269232, Sudbury, Suffolk. Specialist manufacturers and suppliers of clay bricks and tiles.

Blockleys Brick Ltd, 01952 251933, Telford, Shropshire. Supply new bricks.

Opus Property Services, 07816 592124 or 01295 780652. Supply and fit all types of floor tiles, as well as most hardwood and softwood floors, using either new or reclaimed materials.

Anglia Lime Company, 01787 313974, Sudbury, Suffolk. Offer mortar analysis service (by post) and sell lime, lime products and readymix mortars.

AUCTION HOUSES, DEALING WITH ARCHITECTURAL ANTIQUES

(S) Summers Place Auctions, 01403 331331, Billingshurst, Sussex
Christie's South Kensington, 020 7581 7611, London
Gaze and Son, 01379 650306, Diss, Norfolk

ANTIQUE LIGHTING SPECIALISTS

Hector Finch Lighting, 020 7731 8886, London
Kelly Antique Lighting, 01142 678500, Sheffield, South Yorkshire
Josie Marsden, Magic Lanterns at By George, 01727 865680, St Albans, Herts
Christopher Wray, London, 020 7751 8701, London SW6

AUTHOR

The author, Geoffrey David West, has his own website: www.geoffreydavidwest.com.

Index